THE REAL SEINFELD

AS TOLD BY
THE REAL COSTANZA

THE REAL SEINFELD

AS TOLD BY THE REAL COSTANZA
Mike Costanza

with Greg Lawrence

WORDWISE BOOKS
New York, New York

79/.95
COS

First Edition

Library of Congress Catalog Card Number: 98-90230
ISBN: 0-9663298-0-5

Published by WordWise Books, New York, NY

Book design by Lorraine Louie

Distributor to the trade: Access Publishers Network
                              6893 Sullivan Road
                              Grawn, Michigan 49637
                              (616) 276-5196

Printed by: Publishers Press
                              1900 West 2300 South
                              Salt Lake City, Utah 84119
                              (888) 711-1776

To my wife, Marie,
the wind shear beneath my wings.

Acknowledgments

There are many, many people I would like to thank in this space. If I have left anyone out, please forgive me and understand it's just the old memory at fault.

First, I want to thank my wife, Marie, who has been along for a very bumpy ride and found a way to still love me, enjoy what we have and not bother about what we don't. You are the best mother our two wonderful girls, Mariel and Emily, could ever have. I love you very much. Thank you, Jesse Michnick, my great friend of 38 years for the help and advice in writing this book. Your memory of the great times we shared was invaluable, and I treasure your kindness and friendship. Thanks and a big hug to Tony "D" D'Alto for your encouragement and the great photos. I can't thank you enough for your friendship, love and loyalty over the years. I want to thank Greg Lawrence, a person with unshakable faith in this project. You heard my story and instantly understood my need to write this book and push on when the odds were against us. I love you for that, buddy. You are a great writer and also my friend. Thanks also to Julie and Paisley Cencebaugh and Paula Striklin. Thanks to Bonnie Egan, without whose insight, faith, professionalism and financial support, there would not be a book. You pulled a rabbit out of a hat and I will always be grateful for that. My deep thanks to the cast of supporting players in shaping this book: Lorraine Louie, a great designer who came to our rescue, Lydia Grier who created our home page, Melody Lawrence for her expert help editing, Lynne Adams for coaching and the *Seinfeld* fan club on East Third Street, Cheryl Giordano, Gearoid Dolan and Chris Haub. Thanks to my friend, Ken Grimball, News12, Long Island, for his enthusiastic support from the start. To my family, my mother and father and brother, Bobby and his family, I thank you for my heritage and the great Kodak moments. To my brother, Joe, for being one of the thousands of struggling actors who wouldn't think of doing anything else. You are my hero for your determination to follow your heart. Thank you for your love and generosity to me and my family. To Anthony Mannino (Tony) for being my mentor and friend, for believing in me as an actor and a person, and for the honor of writing the forward to your book. I wish you were here to write one for mine. I miss you.

God bless you all.

Finally, I would like to acknowledge my Lord and Savior Jesus Christ whose love and saving grace have taught me that it's never too late to be saved, never too early to do something for someone else and that God, who has begun a good work in me, will see it to its completion.

I want to thank Jerry Seinfeld
for his friendship and support
over the years.
I wish you the very best, Buddy.
God bless you.

Contents

Chapter One

The Curse of Costanza

It was the morning of March 22, 1992, and I was waiting to take off from Kennedy Airport in the middle of a freak snowstorm. The pilot announced that our flight was being held because of the weather, but he didn't tell us that Flight 102 had just crashed at LaGuardia, or that our departure would be delayed for hours. With seatbelt buckled, I sat back helplessly and watched the snow whirl across the runway outside my window. I was starting to panic. It was one of those crazy situations that had me feeling like George Costanza. My namesake. My nemesis. My neurotic alter ego, the character who had been dreamed up a few years before by my pal, Jerry Seinfeld.

How many millions of fans in the vast TV audience identified George as their own bungling Everyman? Yet only one of them could claim to be the real George Costanza as I could. The real George? I'd been cursed—"Costanzarized," as Jerry used to say whenever something would go wrong in my life.

I'd wreck a car—Costanzarized! I'd lose another job—Costanzarized! I'd break up with my girlfriend—Costanzarized! Sometimes he'd see it written on my face and accuse me, "You pulled another Costanza, didn't you, Mikey?" He knew. Jerry always knew, like only your best friend can know, somebody you let all the way into your heart and into your world until you've got no secrets. Somebody you trust like a brother.

With the wings icing and my flight now kiboshed by a fierce nor'easter, I really was pulling another Costanza. I grimaced and muttered aloud, "Son of a bitch...will you look at that snow!

It's been coming down for hours already. When's it gonna stop? I can't believe this. I finally get a part on *Seinfeld*, my big break, and I'm not even gonna make it to L.A. I'm gonna die in a plane crash before I get there! I should've known this was going to happen. Thanks to you, Jerry. I owe you one, buddy."

Looking like an uptight runway model, a flight attendant made her way toward me along the aisle. She stopped short and leaned over the empty seat next to mine, checking the seatback as if she were trying to find whoever I'd been talking to. Catching sight of my bald head, she gave me a quick, nervous smile. Then she started backing away, glancing past me to see out the window.

I asked her, "Are we really gonna fly in this?"

She didn't offer an answer. Nothing but a gorgeous blank face as she turned and hurried down the aisle. Maybe I should have worn my rug on this trip. Or my Yankees cap. Baldism—discrimination against the hairless or hair-impaired. George was right about that one. It's everywhere.

Moments later I was distracted by a noisy commotion in front of me. A couple shouting in a foreign language. Oh, these people, I thought. What is it with them? I'm looking at six hours of non-stop Hungarian! Why is it that people you can't understand always talk so much louder than other people? It's like they're yelling through bullhorns.

The engines were throttled to a dull roar, almost drowning out the Hungarians. My ears were already popping, and we hadn't even taken off. I reached down into my jacket pocket and felt a little audio-tape from my answering machine at home. I could hear Jerry's voice leaving me a phone message three years before, saying, "Mikey, I've named my best friend on the show after you...for everything we've been through...for your love and support. I just wanted you to know..."

We never talked about it, not even after the show aired and George Costanza became a reality playing on bits and pieces of my life. The tape was now a charm for luck, and Jerry's sentiments somehow reassured me under the circumstances.

I'd heard that voice again only a week ago, telling me on

the phone from L.A. "Mikey, I've got a spot for you on the show. You're perfect for it! It's a small part, but you'll be great. Ya gotta fly out here. We can spend some time together."

It wasn't quite as simple as it sounded. I had submitted a videotape of one of my acting roles for the producers and director of the show to approve; and eventually, I borrowed some money from my brother so I could fly to L.A. with only twenty-four hours notice. It was like Jerry had plucked me out of my life, and I was being transported into a whirlwind Hollywood dream.

Though I had been selling real estate for the past couple of years on Long Island, I was also struggling to make it as an actor in Manhattan, going to cattle call auditions and landing occasional commercials and off-Broadway stage roles. The real estate paid the bills, but my life was acting. And, like every actor, I had dreams. So the chance to appear on *Seinfeld* and hang out again with Jerry had seemed at first too good to be true.

But here I was—on a plane lifting into the air through a raging blizzard, hurtling toward certain death. And there was so much on my mind I'd wanted to tell Jerry. I had to explain to him about George—about the way the character was starting to affect my life, which was no joke. This George thing was getting entirely out of hand. People would hear the name, Costanza, and it was like I suddenly had bad breath and the bubonic plague. My wife, Marie, was worried that I was losing real estate clients and acting jobs. She'd made me promise to talk about it with Jerry. Before I left for the airport that morning, she told me, "You need to have a heart-to-heart with him, Mike. He's your friend."

Of course, Jerry had no idea, and I had no idea how to tell him. He'd created the character with the best of intentions. How could I break it to him without hurting his feelings? George had taken on a life of his own.

The Hungarian travelers in front pushed their seats all the way back, trapping me in mine. I soon put George out of mind, and by the time we landed at LAX Airport, having survived the disaster movie of my plane flight, I was more worried about my part on the show than anything else.

My brother, Joe, was an aspiring actor who had just moved to L.A. He put me up at his place that night, and the next morning at ten, he dropped me off at Studio City to meet Jerry. After passing through the security check at the front gate, I followed a sidewalk under palm trees toward the main studio building, passing actors in costumes, and technicians shuttling about with equipment and props, all moving like illusions under a blue canopy of sky. The magical world of Hollywood had now surrounded me, and I was thrilled just to be on the lot.

After entering what appeared to be a modest office building, I gave my name to a receptionist. She was all business and didn't appear to notice anything unusual about my last name. I waited for a few minutes and then Jerry himself came out to greet me. He was effusive and hugged me like he always did. "Mikey, it's good to see you. How are you, buddy?"

"Great, Jerry, great. Except the flight took almost twelve hours. I thought I was a goner."

"Oh, that's right," he bantered with a broad grin, "I heard you had some snow."

I thanked Jerry again for the part on the show, and voiced my concern about doing a good job. "Jerry, I just don't want to give anybody a reason to say to you, 'Hey, Seinfeld, where did you find that guy?'"

Jerry laughed and said, "Oh, you'll be fine. Just relax and be yourself, Mikey."

He made it sound so easy, but I knew that Jerry was a master at being himself, even in his stand-up act, and he worked hard at it for the cameras. As an actor, I appreciated his discipline as well as his phenomenal talent.

The filming of the show was run on a tight schedule. Jerry led me to a nearby conference room and there introduced me to the *Seinfeld* cast and crew members, most of whom were huddled around a large buffet table spread with bagels, muffins, croissants, pastry and coffee. The atmosphere was relaxed and upbeat. I felt as if I'd stepped through a TV screen and landed in the middle of some new episode of the show, one that I hadn't seen yet.

There was Jerry, of course, holding court, along with Julia Louis-Dreyfus as Elaine, Michael Richards as Kramer, Wayne Knight as Newman, and at that moment reaching out to shake my hand, Jason Alexander as George. Jerry repeated my name, and I had the strange feeling of somebody meeting his double for the first time, an eerie doppelgänger from some parallel universe. Jason exuded warmth and put me quickly at ease, saying jovially, "Oh, the real Costanza!"

Julia might have been Elaine with that 24-carat, melt-your-heart smile of hers, saying, "We've heard so much about you!"

Jerry quickly explained that I had just flown into town and was going to be a truck driver with a load of ice cream on today's episode. Then we took seats at a huge conference table to read the script. At the head of the table sat the director, Tom Cherones, an affable, bearded man in a sports jacket. Tom suggested that we get down to business. He was the one who called the shots, listening to us intently and taking notes. Jerry sat next to him, and I sat next to Jerry. The L.A. sun pouring through the windows seemed to make the whole room glitter.

One question was echoing in my mind: *What am I doing here?*

I was lightheaded, giddy, jet-lagged, and star-struck all at once, and still sweating some nervous bullets about my part. What if I were to pull a Costanza and embarrass Jerry? The episode was called "The Parking Space," and the story involved a fight between George and one of Kramer's friends over a parking place which both happened to go for at the same time. I played a truck driver who became outraged when their scuffle snarled traffic on the street and blocked his way.

Waiting for my turn to read, I wondered how I would work up any anger in the pleasant environment in which I now found myself. Nevertheless, when the time finally came, I delivered my "Hey, get out of the way" lines with such enthusiastic ferocity that Michael Richards, staying in character as Kramer, suddenly leaped up from his seat and shouted with eyes bulging, "Yeow! You better watch out. This man is intense!"

The rest of the cast cracked up at Michael's antics, and my own laughter broke the tension for me, making me feel at home for the first time. I quickly came to understand the group effort on the show had but one goal, the same one Jerry had pursued his whole life: to make us laugh.

For the next four days, I was a member of the family, picked up each morning and taken to the set by Wayne Knight, who was such a buoyant, good-natured fellow compared to his insidious character, the despicable lout, Newman. With Jerry's breakneck schedule, most of the time we had to spend together was on the set, and usually in the company of other actors. Still, we managed to catch each other up during breaks, recalling old times and our mutual friends while standing around waiting for lighting cues, or occasionally taking in a quick gourmet meal at the commissary.

At the end of our first day together on the set, Jerry said, "You see, Mikey, our lives aren't so different. We get up, we go to work, and we go home to bed. Tomorrow we get up and do it all over again. Our lives are essentially the same."

He sounded like he might have been doing one of his *Seinfeld* bits. I pointed out that there were a few minor differences in our bank accounts and marital status. Then I asked him, "So when are you going down?"

That was part of the guy thing, the code we had used between us since our college days—*going down* meant getting married. He just laughed at my question and shook his head, then gave me one of those exasperated "Jerry" looks that said it all. Nothing serious. He wasn't seeing anybody special. The bemused bachelor.

As we parted that night, I teased him again, "Sooner or later you're gonna take the big fall, Seinfeld. The right one will come along someday. Oh yeah, you'll go down. Mark my words."

I had to laugh every time I walked across the living room set of Jerry's "Manhattan" apartment. I marveled at the props, seeing a personal touch in the magnetic ornaments on the refrigerator, and the boxes of cereal that he still loved. I always had the sense of déjà vu in that room, like I was visiting his old apartment on West 81st Street, hanging out with Jerry again, just shooting the breeze with our old gang. Of course, the faces had changed; the old gang was now being portrayed by a group of talented actors, many of whom had living counterparts in the real world of Jerry's past, as well as in the equally real world of Jerry's imagination. It was like he'd somehow recreated all of the personalities and madcap comic moments of his life and put them on his show, with the various scenes and sets all housed in one giant studio hangar.

On the morning of my third day, I found a seat behind the lights and cameras, and watched a scene between Jerry and Elaine being rehearsed on the living room set. Elaine was telling Jerry how a roving gang of teenagers had been chasing her and George in Jerry's car—an outlandish story Elaine had invented to explain away the little car accident that Jerry was going to have to pay for. The crew and cast were having a great time with this one.

The real Jerry was in high spirits. During one of the breaks, he came over and sparred with me. It was like the scene had moved across the living room to include me in the story. Jerry asked how my acting career was going these days, and I saw an opening to bring up the touchy subject that had been troubling me. Trying to be lighthearted about it, I told him, "Well, I had this commercial audition a couple weeks ago, and they told my agent they wanted a 'Costanza-type.' So I figured how can I miss! I'm the real Costanza, aren't I? This is gonna be money in the bank. If there ever was a role that I was born to play, this was it."

Jerry chimed in, "Sure. Perfect for you."

"Right," I said. "A piece of cake."

"The role of a lifetime." He could see it coming. "So what happened?" he asked.

"My agent told me they went with somebody else. I might be the real Costanza but they wanted the other Costanza! I'm cursed, Jerry. I can't book a commercial even when they're looking for me. It's like George has..."

Jerry cut in, "So you didn't book the spot?"

"No."

Trying to humor me, he continued the sparring match, putting on his lawyer act, "And you felt humiliated?"

"Right."

"Ashamed?"

"Yeah."

"Like a loser?"

"Yeah, a real loser."

"And are you going to put yourself through anymore auditions like that?"

Still playing along, I said, "Of course!"

"Ah-ha!" cried Jerry, now standing over me in triumph. "That sounds like the real Costanza to me. I rest my case."

Our laughter was cut short, as Jerry was called back to work on the scene. There was never enough time with him, and the comedy always seemed to blot out the reality. He gave me a light slap on the back, then walked to the set like he owned the place, which he did, of course. I watched him clowning with a stagehand and felt just the slightest twinge of envy.

I repeated our conversation for my wife, Marie, on the phone that night. She wanted to know every detail, and I had to confess that I was disappointed so far. "It wasn't the right situation to get into it," I told her. "It's not easy to talk to him sometimes. Anyway, I'm trying to concentrate on the role. I can't let Jerry down."

Before we hung up, my wife teased me, suggesting in a half-serious tone that Jerry should make me into a regular on the show. A recurring role. I knew that was an impossible dream, but her wishing found its way briefly into a corner of my mind.

* * *

There would be no moment of truth. No startling revelation. No contract offer from NBC. As Costanza, I was lucky to get the job done without being struck down by lightning from the heavens.

My scene was an exterior, a busy street which was shot on

a fabricated New York City set with remarkably realistic store-fronts and sidewalks. I was filmed late in the afternoon of my fourth day before a live audience seated outside on bleachers. I had my lines down cold by this time, and the scene needed only one take, which struck me as totally anticlimactic after spending so many hours rehearsing and preparing each day.

Suddenly, it was all in the can, and I was saying my first round of good-byes.

Michael Richards had taken time to befriend me during the course of my visit, at one point confiding a serious ambition to lecture on the college circuit, such a far cry from the slapstick buffoonery I associated with him. Physical comedy was his passion and the two of us hit it off from the start. When I told him this was my last day, Michael encouraged me to stick around. "You're a natural at this stuff, Mike. You really oughta stay out here and try for a pilot." He said all of this with only a hint that he was, after all, Kramer, the outrageous schemer.

Looking on as members of the crew started breaking down the set, I did my best to hide the sadness in my voice, "No, I can't stay, Michael. I fly back to New York tonight. I've got my wife and family to go home to."

Michael clapped me on the back and said warmly, "You've got family here now too. It's been great working with you, Mike."

After he left, I walked back and loitered inside the studio, waiting until almost everybody else had gone. As if on cue, Jason Alexander and Jerry came to bid me farewell in tandem, like the tag team they created on the show, George and Jerry. The work had gone well, and they were both pleased. I knew that I'd be seeing Jerry again back in New York. Like always, after he finished the season, but still I had a great throbbing lump in my throat.

"You know I love you, pal," I told him. "Thanks for the job."

"You were great out there, Mike," he said graciously, with an arm around my shoulder. "You gave me everything that I could have hoped for. I'll see you back in the city the next time I get home. We'll hang out and play some ball."

9

With that, he was gone. In four days, I had been unable to find the right moment to talk with him about the things that were really weighing on my mind. And now, for the time being at least, the opportunity had passed. I called a taxi and waited by myself for a few minutes in the shadows of a dark *Seinfeld* living room, then quietly left the set for the last time.

The next day I was back in New York City, savoring the irony of the experience with bittersweet emotion, and looking with fresh eyes at the familiar places and the old haunts where it all began, as if it were actually possible to relive our past and rediscover the show behind the show.

It was a feeling that I couldn't shake for years, especially on Thursday nights, when my wife would remind me that *Seinfeld* was on, and we would watch again faithfully in our Long Island living room after putting the kids to bed—almost afraid to find out what unexpected mischief George was going to bring into our lives this week.

Chapter Two

Masters of Our Domain

The real Jerry was a guy I met one afternoon in the fall of 1974 at a friend's house in Queens—a naive Jewish kid from the shopping mall mecca of eastern Long Island. In his case, at least part of the myth was true: Jerry had grown up on Superman, Abbott and Costello routines, and Pez. The only son of a commercial sign-painter, Jerry wore giant, silver-rimmed glasses and often displayed a wry, sometimes wicked, sense of humor. The two of us were urban undergrads; our roving domain and turf-rights stretched from the playgrounds and parking lots of the Queens College campus to the electric wonderland of Manhattan. We weren't really masters of anything in those days, but we had our fantasies.

Jerry was a year ahead of me in school, and he had recently transferred to Queens from Oswego. I kept hearing about him from my friend, Jesse Michnick, another Jewish student who, like Jerry, was majoring in communications. Jesse was the matchmaker who set us up. He told me about a new student I should meet, a seriously funny guy, according to Jesse. He engineered several attempts to introduce us on campus, but Jerry and I kept standing each other up, as if backing out of a blind date.

It was an unlikely match, like trying to mix meatballs and matzo balls. Jerry came from the respectable suburbs, having moved at ten with his family from Brooklyn to Massapequa. My background had me running through the back streets of Queens with second and third generation Sicilians, many of whom were aspiring goodfellas. The Godfather mystique was becoming fashionable and inspired my role models.

After entering college, I was the guy to see on campus for basketball and football tickets, making bets, and buying special discount items that had fallen off the back of a truck. I might have dropped out, but I followed my better instincts, and some of the alluring coeds, into the theater. I threw myself into acting and cast myself as a class clown, always looking for and usually finding a good time or a wild party. My friends called me "Mr. Excitement," and that gave me something to live up to. I really was serious about drama, having first caught the acting bug in junior high.

The fateful meeting with Jerry eventually took place in the basement playroom of Jesse's parents' house. This was in the fall, not long after school had started; as it happened, the three of us had some time to kill between classes that day. Jesse's father was a World War II veteran, and a somewhat eccentric collector of antique clocks and war memorabilia. The Michnick house looked like a cross between a museum and a fun house—a two-story, brick fortress not far from my family's house in the Middle Village section of Queens. At the time, all three of us still lived at home and commuted to school.

Jesse and I were lounging in the downstairs playroom when Jerry arrived on the scene. He gave me the impression of a full-fledged, card-carrying nerd, gaping and wide-eyed behind his glasses. He couldn't help but notice on his way in that the living room and basement were filled from floor to ceiling with clocks— dozens of them, some ticking, some without hands or faces and none of them showing the right time. After the initial introduction had been made between us, the first thing Jerry said was, "How do you guys ever know what time it is around here?"

Proud of his timeless bat cave, Jesse explained to Jerry that whenever anyone really had to know what time it was, the Michnick family consulted the clock on the stove in the kitchen. Jesse was the drummer for a rock band that performed at weddings and bar mitzvahs on weekends. He was a smooth operator and enjoyed playing the role of host in this situation. Like the social coordinator on a cruise ship, he tried to break the ice for us, opening a glass cabinet and pulling out one of several Nazi swords that his father brought back from the war. I watched Jerry's eyes go wide again as Jesse playfully swung the wicked blade in the air under our noses.

"Now check this out," said Jesse. He returned the sword to the cabinet, then removed several jagged pieces of shrapnel from a small drawer, along with a set of false teeth. Jesse wound a key in the back of the teeth. After a flourish, he held them clacking in his hand—a magician's trick. He offered this curious item to Jerry saying, "Here. Watch out you don't lose a finger!" Jerry hefted the teeth in his hand, and they continued to chatter under his nose. He had his head bent over as if he were smelling a rose.

Jesse and I had been pals since grade school, and I had seen Mr. Michnick's collection many times. It entered my mind that for Jerry these keepsakes from another world would probably come across like a trip to the Twilight Zone. There was a moment of silence as Jesse and I sized him up. He had a strange expression on his face, a mischievous sort of deadpan. He finally looked up and asked me with schoolboy innocence, "Do you think this guy was still alive when Mr. Michnick took these?"

As soon as his words registered, Jesse and I cracked up, and the friendship took off from there, quickly escalating into madcap imitations of The Three Stooges. There was an edge to our clowning and camaraderie—one-upmanship played to the hilt. We spent some time recounting bits of trivia from classic Humphrey Bogart movies, and then decided to head back to school. We were running late, and Jerry complained how hard it was going to be to get a parking place near campus. The parking situation was a full-blown obsession for all of us. When we were leaving Jesse's house, I casually handed Jerry a campus parking pass.

"Where did you get this?" Jerry asked.

Jesse told him, "You don't want to know."

Jerry looked at the pass warily, and then at me, like I had given him a ticket into some forbidden world. He asked Jesse, "Is it real?"

Jesse shook his head and told him again, "Jerry, you don't

want to know."

Without asking more questions, Jerry thanked me and put the bootleg pass in his car, then drove away, obviously thrilled with the prospect of parking on campus. This was the guy thing again, that unwritten code for being cool, with all its complex laws and by-laws. What else did we guys have to guide us on our way into the uncertain terrain of relationships?

I looked at the gesture with the pass as a good deed and was pleased with myself, like any nineteen-year-old would be when his ego is temporarily able to overcome his insecurities. The episode seemed frivolous; yet I knew that I had won Jerry's respect and made a new friend.

Even with passes, parking places were still difficult to find at Queens College. The hunt for the "perfect spot" soon became one of our ongoing sports—pursued with the same intensity with which we played baseball and flew kites in Juniper Valley Park around the corner from Jesse's place. My ability to parallel park was legendary among my friends even before I knew Jerry. Sometimes he accused me of lifting my car by crane into particularly tight spots, insisting there could be no other physical explanation for how I had managed to squeeze in, aside from levitation.

Parking meters were out of the question. Long before George ever delivered his first line, I took part in endless "philosophical" debates with Jerry, often while we searched side streets for a choice parking place. I enjoyed poking fun at his proper middle-class views with my more jaded, streetwise cynicism. As far as putting quarters into a meter, I harped on one point to him in particular: "Why should you pay for anything that you can get free?" Years later George would embellish this simple principle with a punch line likening the parking meter to a prostitute. It seemed like common sense to me.

Jerry was the mild-mannered, straight arrow of our screwball gang, our own self-styled rat pack, and I was pleased to take him under my wing. I liked having a friend with a killer wit who came from the right side of the tracks. In my mind, the new friendship seemed to confirm that I was traveling in the right direction with my life, as the first of my family to attend college and pursue a goal that went beyond a trade, or any of the less noble careers that some others in the neighborhood had fallen into.

Of course, I would never have told any of this to Jerry back then, not even after we started hanging out on a daily basis. The open admission of affection to a guy friend would have broken the code, which, like *omerta*, demanded silence.

For his part, whenever we were together, he loved to taunt, tease, cajole, mock, and heckle me—all in good fun, though the joke was usually on me or at my expense. He would tell me, "Mikey, you're the only person I know who risks his life speeding to arrive someplace just so he can leave." Or he would say, "You're the kind of guy who turns around to avoid traffic and drives the wrong way just to keep moving." Pizza was a major staple for both of us, and Jerry liked to nail me for my healthy appetite: "Costanza, you're the first person I've ever known who can eat a whole pizza while waiting for a slice to go."

That was the way his mind worked—observing, analyzing and dissecting every scene and personality. His observations about my behavior and habits were often right on the mark, hilariously and sometimes painfully so.

Little did any of us know back then that he was collecting material.

* * *

My neighborhood was a section of Middle Village, like Little Italy in some ways, though there was more space between the houses, each with its own lot. Many of the families were Italian-Americans and used their backyards and front stoops as gathering places where stories and gossip of the day could be exchanged. The neighborhood had its share of colorful and bizarre characters; they soon became a fascination for Jerry, who would visit me at home after school or between classes. At first, we made only quick stops for snacks in my mother's kitchen or held brief meetings in the living room, as this budding friendship between us guys had to progress step-by-step through the required phases, like a romance.

I remember one afternoon, not long after we first met, when Jerry stopped in and I told him about my new job. I was working nights as a bouncer in a gay bar on Queens Boulevard. This was the first in a string of jobs that I would work over the years, only to be fired or to quit—as if fate had chosen me to prepare George's future resume for him. I broke the news about my new bar job while we sat in the Costanza living room. Jerry was flabbergasted when he heard where I was working. I explained somewhat defensively, "It fits my schedule. I'm tellin' ya, it's perfect."

Tilting back in my father's recliner, Jerry suddenly jolted forward and asked me point blank, "But what exactly does a bouncer in a gay bar do? What can this job entail? Do you break up fights between drag queens when they start insulting each other's make-up? What? You try to keep them from dishing each other? I mean, Mike, is there really any need for a bouncer in a gay place? I have to tell you the whole thing sounds very strange. Not that I doubt your word..."

I explained to him that the purpose of my job was to keep straight people out of the bar. No heteros allowed. I told him, "I stay on the lookout. You have to be able to recognize straight guys who wander in by mistake. I usually watch for the expressions on their faces when they first come through the door—you know, when they see a hundred and fifty guys standing around wearing leather and jewelry."

In reality, I met a diverse crowd of people on the job and no one ever gave me a hard time for being the only straight male in the place. The bar was owned by Uncle Sal, one of my neighbors who wasn't really related to me but had treated me as family ever since I was a kid. I told Jerry that Uncle Sal was rumored to be a made man, a Mafia big shot, who just happened to own the gay bar along with a few after-hours clubs.

Jerry said in a lighthearted tone, "That doesn't make him a member of the Mafia, does it? How do crazy rumors like that get started anyway?" He made the same sort of offhanded quips about his neighbor, Carlo Gambino, who, coincidentally, lived only a stone's throw away from the Seinfelds' home on Long Island.

In Uncle Sal's case, the rumors were started whenever he went away, or whenever he was said to be on "vacation" by his neighbors, some of whom had read in the papers that he had been sentenced and sent up to prison for so many counts of racketeering and extortion. But he really was a charming fellow, and Jerry loved to hear about him, sometimes pumping me for stories that he would have me repeat over and over.

On this day, to make the case, I showed Jerry the palatial manor at the end of the block where Uncle Sal lived. On a street of narrow, semi-detached homes, two houses looked out of place, and both belonged to Uncle Sal. The front of one looked like the Roman Coliseum. There were marble columns and a fountain with the statue of a cherub spitting water into a basin. The entrance was a steel and stained glass monstrosity framed in a portal. This villa was attached to Uncle Sal's other house next door by a wrought iron gate with spikes, as if daring anyone to climb over.

As we walked by to do a little spying, I told Jerry, "All the windows are bulletproof."

"How do you know?" he asked, keeping his voice down. Peering in at Uncle Sal's compound, the two of us might have looked like we were planning a break-in.

"Trust me," I said. "The people who hang out around here are straight out of *The Valachi Papers*. I'm not kidding. They ride up in Cadillac limos and strut their stuff in the yard. You gotta see these guys!" I pointed out a German shepherd patrolling behind the fence and a surveillance camera mounted over the gate. We decided not to push our luck.

As we walked back up the street to my house, I said to Jerry, "You should see his basement. It's like the wildest disco you can imagine. Wall-to-wall smoked glass, and a twenty-foot mahogany bar with disco balls and a crystal chandelier hanging from the ceiling. You should have been here on the fourth of July when Sal put in his fireplace..."

"You were in there?" asked Jerry, incredulously. "You were inside?"

"Sure. He had about sixty people over. I was there early before anyone else arrived. He put in this fieldstone fireplace that covered the whole wall. The guy is unreal! He turns up the air conditioning, and then he lights a fire on the hottest day of the summer...just so the guests could roast marshmallows! Almost burned the place down. You should have been there, Jerry. You could have met Sally Balls and Willie Thirty-Eight—two very sweet guys."

"I'm sure," said Jerry. "How did they get their names?"

"You don't want to know," I told him.

Several months later I introduced Jerry to Carmine Thirty-Eight, who was actually no relation to Willie. They didn't even know each other. Carmine hung out in a social club that was near my old school, Grover Cleveland High School (where my gym teacher, Mr. Sirota, had twisted my last name years before and nicknamed me, "Can't-Stand-Ya," a true story that Jerry would one day ascribe to George on the show). The club was called The Club, and had the atmosphere of an old Greenwich Village coffee shop with expresso machines, and faded murals that tried to make you feel like you were someplace in Italy or Greece.

Jerry and I loved to play jokes on unsuspecting souls, and Carmine was a perfect patsy. A fun-loving guy from Brooklyn, he was good-natured and slightly dull-witted. According to Jerry, he looked like the Slip Mahoney character from the classic East Side Gang comedy team. He was one of the regulars and always occupied the same stool at the club, and that was where Jerry and I found him. It was a spring night, and we were on our way to a Yankee game.

As we said hello and swung around him, Carmine caught Jerry's elbow and asked, in thick Brooklynese, "Hey, where you guys goin'? Out to play with the goils?"

Jerry gave me an eye roll and said, "No, the Yankees. We're on our way to the game."

Carmine was gassed up. He said to me, "Oh, you're goin'

to the game! Mikey, did I ever tell ya I was a minor league umpire?"

"No, Carmine," I said. "I never heard that one. Why don't you tell us."

"Yeah, sure, I was an ump for many years. Had a few close calls with death."

"Oh, really?" asked Jerry, raising his eyebrows.

"Yeah, sure," said Carmine, working all his facial muscles into a serious expression that made him look like a human cartoon. "Very dangerous job callin' balls and strikes. Very dangerous."

He was dying to tell us, and Jerry encouraged him, asking, "How dangerous could it be, Carmine?"

"Oh, many a game I was behind the plate, and the fans didn't like my calls. Yeah, sure, many times I had to be escorted outta the park. Very rough crowds back then. Very rough."

Carmine accepted our laughter graciously. This was his show, and he drew the attention of a small crowd. He grabbed hold of my wrist, saying, "Mike, come here. I gotta ask ya something. I see ya out with the goils all the time. How do ya do it? What's your secret?"

I shot a look to Jerry, tipping him off. "Should I tell him, Jer?"

Playing along, Jerry said, "I don't know, Mike. He might not be ready for this."

I looked at Carmine and held back. He pleaded, "Aw, come on, Mike, ya gotta tell me."

"Okay, Carmine," I said. "But you can't tell anybody. Not a soul."

"Sure, Mike, sure. You can trust me."

I heard Jerry saying under his breath, "I can't wait to hear this one."

Some of the onlookers pressed closer to hear. I put an arm around Carmine's shoulder and allowed the tension to build through a few more heartbeats. Then I told him, "Mayonnaise. That's the secret. Very few people know."

Carmine shook his head in bewilderment. "Mayonnaise?

What the hell you talkin' about, Mike?" He turned to Jerry and said, "He's kiddin' me, right?"

Keeping a straight face, Jerry assured him that I was serious. We knew we had him going now, and I kept it up mercilessly. "Girls go crazy for the stuff. You keep a jar in the glove compartment of your car. When you're out on a date and the right moment comes, you take it out. Ba-boom! Works every time."

"Yeah, sure," said Carmine. "Mayonnaise, huh?"

"Have I ever lied to you, Carmine?" I offered some graphic instructions, and then goaded him, "Just try it the next time you go out, Carmine. No girl can resist mayonnaise. You'll have her eating out of your hand."

By the time Jerry and I left for the game, Carmine had become a true believer. Jerry and I spent nine innings at Yankee Stadium that night repeating the line, "Yeah, sure, many times I had to be escorted outta the park." Years after the incident, either one of us could get a laugh from the other on any occasion just by saying, "Yeah, sure, many times..."

But the punch line came two days later, when Jerry and I went back to the club and saw Carmine again. He flagged us down as soon as we stepped inside, yelling, "Hey, Mike, that secret you told me was a lotta bull! Didn't work."

Jerry said in my ear, "Here we go again..."

I asked Carmine, "What happened? You tried the mayo?"

Carmine said, "Yeah, I tried it, just like you said. I took a goil out drivin' and I did everything you said. I pull over and park in a nice spot, ya know, and we're kissin' and playin' around, gettin' pretty hot'n'heavy. So I take the jar of mayonnaise outta the glove compartment. Then I says, 'Sweetheart, are you ready for the mayonnaise?' She says 'What mayonnaise?' And I'm all ready to dab some on her thighs, y'know? Well, she gets outta the car like she's mad, and says to me, 'What do I look like, a turkey sandwich?'"

Both Jerry and I busted a gut, then offered our apologies to poor Carmine.

* * *

My house was much closer to Queens College than Jerry's home out on Long Island, and so I was a geographically desirable friend to have. He stopped in more and more often, eventually staying for dinner and meeting the rest of my family. My father, Joe Costanza, was a hardworking printer, and a member of the union all his life; my mother, Millie, was a tireless homemaker. As second generation Italians, my parents did their best to lay claim to a piece of the American dream while bringing me and my two younger brothers, Joe and Bobby, into the world. My brothers were in high school when Jerry started coming around.

Like George's parents on *Seinfeld*, my parents carried on a high-pitched, continual screaming match day and night, quarreling over every imaginable subject as if performing on the stage of some opera house. Even a simple request to pass the bread at the dinner table could turn my father into a raging Pavarotti, and my mother's inspired shrieks were high enough to shatter glass. Having no idea what to expect, even with my advance warnings, Jerry got quite a dose of the Costanzas the first time he visited.

I had a huge bedroom in our finished basement that was my fortress of solitude, and that was where I brought Jerry on that distant afternoon. I led him down the basement stairs and showed him my room, with pictures on the wall of Frank Sinatra and Mickey Mantle. There was a small daybed where I slept, and it was dwarfed by a full-size nightclub bar, which my parents kept stocked. Music was mandatory and I had the Beatles playing on my old eight-track sound system as we walked in, knowing that Jerry was a fan. We had already spent a lot of hours hanging out together, but bringing my friend to my room meant that we were turning a corner into really serious paldom. It was like an initiation rite into this exotic Italian tribe, and I was just curious to see how Jerry would react.

The first thing that caught his eye was a winepress that my father kept in the basement laundry room. We had a grape arbor in the backyard, and my father made his own wine each year, a

Costanza tradition. After touring my lair, Jerry and I confirmed our shared musical tastes, listening to some tunes from the Rolling Stones and Led Zeppelin. We were typical 70's guys: wearing bell-bottoms and T-shirts, talking movies and cars and girls. We discovered common interests, ranging from theater and sports to conspiracy theories about the JFK assassination. Watergate and Vietnam were recent memories; we were cynics when it came to politics.

Jerry had a steady girlfriend at the time, Karen Trager, a studious coed from Long Island. Karen transferred the same year from Oswego to be near him; he was deeply in love with her in the sense of those wild feelings that only the first serious romance of anyone's life can inspire. I came to realize after knowing him for a while that Jerry kept girls in a special compartment of his life. The guy territory was a separate, sacred domain most of the time, even later when we double-dated or ventured into singles scenes during our stag nights out on the town.

Our bonding ritual in my bedroom was briefly interrupted when we heard the first act of the screeching, operatic mayhem which was getting underway upstairs between my parents. At that point, Jerry asked me to leave him alone for twenty minutes so he could meditate on the daybed. I asked about meditation, and he explained that it involved breathing and concentrating on his mantra. It was a new one on me.

"Mantra?" I said.

He told me, "It's like listening to a sound that's only in your mind. You should try it sometime, Mike. Really. It could help you relax and focus your energy..."

I knew he wasn't suggesting some mystical trick, but that he realized I took acting very seriously and that meditation might be something that I could use in the theater. I had encouraged Jerry to take some classes in the drama department, and later, we enrolled in drama classes together. We wrote several skits, including a commercial for Baskin Robbins Ice Cream that was a raucous spoof of *The Godfather*. We also created a Crazy Eddie routine, where we pitched sex rather than discount stereo systems, and our prices were insane! There was nothing that either of us wouldn't try to make some funny bit work, whether we were writing or just playing around. It was the one thing that both of us were serious about, each in his own way, from the beginning.

Leaving Jerry to meditate on the daybed, I ran upstairs to check when dinner would be ready. I found my father and brothers hovering around the kitchen table, where my mother was preparing a huge pot of *pasta e fagioli*. I asked her, "Did you make anything besides the pasta, Ma?"

My father jumped in with his usual ferocity. "Your mother made eggplant. Now call your friend to the table! It's time to eat!"

My brother, Joe, complained under his breath, "I'll eat the eggplant, but I'm not touching that pasta."

"Since when?" I asked.

Overhearing him, my father rapped the table with his knuckles, saying loudly, "You eat whatever your mother makes, or you won't eat in this house!"

My mother said, her high-pitched voice quavering, "What? You all have particular palates now? Well, this is what we have to eat tonight! If it's not good enough for you, you cook something else. Michael, go get your friend."

Deciding at the same moment to bring up some soda from the basement bar, my father pushed ahead and beat me down the stairs, where he found Jerry sitting on the daybed with his eyes closed. As my father and I stood there looking at him, I said in a low voice, "He's meditating, Pop. He'll be done in a minute."

"What meditating?" my father said loudly. "He's out like a light!"

My father retrieved a bottle of his favorite Kula White Rock Pineapple Soda from the bar, then passed me on his way back up the stairs, saying, "Your friend looks like a corpse. Ya better find out what's wrong with him."

As soon as my father had gone, Jerry came out of his trance, laughing and springing up from the daybed. He tried to imitate my father's voice, saying, "Well, I've just learned this new mantra: pasta fazool, eh?"

On our way up the stairs, he asked me, "Am I ready for this, Mike? Is there anything else I should know?"

I stopped on the top step and said, "Just make sure you wait till my father takes his food, and when you get down to the white part, that's the plate..."

Moments later as we stepped into the dining room to join the rest of my family, Jerry grabbed my elbow and whispered in my ear, "Who's the Illustrated Man?"

He meant my youngest brother, Bobby, a teenage body-builder wearing a muscle man T-shirt, showing off his arms and shoulders that were covered with tattoos. As Jerry and I stood in front of the table, I made the introductions. Then we took our seats, and my father tried to make a joke in his usual gruff way, "It's nice to meet you, Jerry, but I have to tell you, if you're gonna sleep here, we'll have to charge you extra. You were only invited for dinner."

My mother said, "Leave the boy alone, Joe. He comes from a nice Jewish family, isn't that right, Jerry?"

Jerry gave her a wan smile and said, "That's right, Mrs. Costanza."

My mother continued, "I always wanted my son to have better friends..."

My father cut her off, "That's enough! Let's eat! Millie, serve our guest first."

"Are you tryin' to tell me what to do, Joe?" My mother held a giant serving spoon in her hand and waggled it at my father, as she added, "Because I know what to do!" She filled Jerry's plate with eggplant, then asked, "Eggplant, Jerry?"

At the same time, my father filled Jerry's glass with Kula White Rock Pineapple Soda, then said brusquely, "Have some soda, Jerry."

Jerry, who was already a bit of a health fanatic with very fastidious eating habits, never had a chance to protest—he was now a full-fledged member of the Costanza tribe. The hospitality included forced-feeding and, to his credit, Jerry never lost his sense of humor about it.

After dinner, we escaped back to the basement and had a few laughs. Jerry waited around while I answered nature's call and did my usual routine in the bathroom—my "home base"—where it was always my habit to take off my clothes, all of my clothes. So when I came out, I was more or less naked except for a recent issue of *Sports Illustrated* that I was holding in my hand.

Jerry took one look at me and said, "Okay, Costanza, let's have it..."

"What?" I said.

"You must have some explanation for walking out here like that. What happened? You fell in the bathtub with your clothes on?"

I said, "What?...Oh." The blush on my face felt like a bad sunburn. "I like to take off my clothes in the bathroom. It's a matter of comfort—I make myself comfortable when I'm in there! It's the only place where I have total privacy, so I go all out. What's so funny about that, Seinfeld?"

He was doubled over, and the laughter soon became contagious. Apparently, that image was indelibly etched in Jerry's mind. Years later he would haunt me with it—by having George Costanza emerge from the bathroom either shirtless or tripping over his pants for an audience of millions.

What else are friends for?

* * *

The cultural exchange between me and Jerry worked two ways. For every meatball there was a matzo ball—or milk and chocolate chip cookies—which was what Jerry's mother, Betty, served me on a tray whenever I would drive out and visit the Seinfelds' home in Massapequa. Jerry's father, Kalman, who went by Kal, had a warm sense of humor, and there was a hint of Jerry in his manner. As a sign-maker, Kal was a printer, like my father; but that was where any similarity between our families ended. The Seinfeld household always seemed very civilized and quiet compared to the Costanza three-ring circus.

While I introduced Jerry to the exotic quirks of my Sicilian heritage, he taught me how to play the Israeli paddle game Kadima. He somehow even inspired me to attend a Jewish singles mixer in Brooklyn (some readers will remember that Kramer as a "goy" experienced a similar folly on the show). After I returned from the mixer, I griped to Jerry that I wasn't able to get any girls to dance. He said, "Well, Mikey, you might have had better luck if you had worn a yarmulke."

I told him, "You know, it was supposed to be a *yeshiva* mixer. Doesn't that sound Italian to you?"

We were inseparable. We spent an unhealthy amount of time frequenting diners and restaurants all over Queens, and going to movies, or waiting on line to get into movies like *Star Wars*, and driving our cars. In the fall of 1976, Jerry convinced me to buy a new Fiat, the kind of car that both he and his sister, Carolyn, drove. I had already destroyed at least fifteen cars by the time I met Jerry, and he believed that a new car would have a better chance of surviving me as a driver than the junkers I was used to. There was only one problem with a Fiat—I didn't know how to drive a stick shift.

"There's nothing to it," Jerry assured me. "I'll have you driving a stick in an hour."

This seemingly simple task turned out to be far more of a nightmarish ordeal than either of us ever imagined. Rather than give me lessons in his car, he wisely insisted that we wait until the afternoon that I picked up my new wheels from the dealer. A gorgeous, powder blue Fiat 131. I bought it from Nemet Fiat on Hillside Avenue in Queens. "You're gonna love this car," said Jerry, as he drove it off the lot for me.

We went to one of the empty parking lots at Juniper Valley Park where I got behind the wheel and then spent all of about ten minutes practicing on the stick shift. I announced to Jerry, "I'm ready for the streets! Let's take a spin over to Jesse's house. I want him to see the car."

"Are you sure you're ready, Mikey?" Jerry asked, with some trepidation in his voice.

"Nothing to it," I said.

I took off burning rubber and subjecting us both to instant whiplash. When I looked over at him, his face was contorted like he was on the roller coaster ride of his life, and had just gone into the big dip.

As we swerved into oncoming traffic, Jerry screamed at me, "Clutch, brake...stop! Clutch, brake...stop!"

He repeated those words a number of times on our little trip, like another mantra he had learned. After we finally pulled up on the street in front of Jesse's place, he leaped out of the car like a gazelle, then just stood on the curb shaking his head. I laughed until there were tears in my eyes as I watched him walk all the way around the car making a big deal out of checking for damage. After I got out, he told me, "Now I know why the cars back up as soon as they see you walk into the showroom...I hate to have to tell you, pal, but you already put a dent on the roof. Have a look."

"No way!" I said.

"How do you do it, Mikey? How does someone destroy the roof of a car the first time he gets behind the wheel?"

I wasn't worried. It was only a little scratch, just another ding on the road of life.

When we walked up the steps to Jesse's front door, Jerry said, "Only you, Costanza. Only you."

Seven months later I blew the engine, and my new car days were over.

* * *

Our social lives more and more revolved around the theater. I was cast in quite a few college plays, and Jerry always came to see me in the shows. Even though Jerry hadn't done any acting, he was into drama and actors. We had an ongoing argument over who was better, DeNiro or Pacino; and from year to year, we switched sides in this debate as each came out in new movies. Waiting on lines at theaters or waiting to be seated (sometimes hours) at our favorite Chinatown restaurants, Jerry would offer some riotous imitations and bits of mimicry just to pass the time.

He was great to have in the audience. During my junior year, when I performed the role of Chuckles in *A Thousand Clowns*, I heard Jerry's familiar cackles and snickers throughout the show, cheering me on at every funny moment, like he was trying to single-handedly provide me with a laugh track. Afterwards, he amused himself by imitating me when we took dates to dinner in Manhattan. We went to the Mandarin Inn on Mott Street, and it was a memorable occasion if only because in the midst of our little celebration, Jerry finally gave in to my prodding, and said that he was going to try out for the next student production.

He leaned across the table and told me, "I'm gonna audition for *Cuckoo's Nest*. What do you think, Mike?"

"That's a great play for you," I said. "It's about time you put your ass on the boards, Seinfeld."

That was it. The announcement went by without much comment from the girls, but I knew that he had given this decision plenty of thought because he had apparently overcome his fear of taking that big step onto the stage.

Jerry had brought his steady squeeze, Karen, and I had taken out an actress from the cast. As Jerry liked to remind me, I went through girls almost as quickly as I went through cars, and my luck in this regard had become a source of endless hilarity for him. He and Karen would provide the witty repartee and moral support for me whenever we double-dated and I would bring along some new candidate in the romantic interest department. The two of them enabled me to be myself without the normal, crippling anxieties of being alone on a first date ("going one-on-one" as we called it). At the end of the night, Jerry would privately give me the thumbs-up or thumbs-down, usually the latter. Wit, rather than looks, counted above all else to him, no matter how I argued that one could compensate for the other.

Jerry eventually immortalized our early odd-couple, double-dating rituals through our televised alter egos. But at the time, we were just doing what came naturally. It was understood that no guy would ever give up another guy to a girl. No guy would snitch behind another's back—such a betrayal was unthinkable. We took all of this seriously enough to joke about it, knowing our bizarre code of male honor was as close as either of us was ever going to get to living the life of a loyal mob soldier, or superhero, or heavy-weight champ.

After a guy dated someone for more than a week, the typical exchange in our circle of friends often ran something like this:

"So, you're seein' what's-her-name tonight?"

"Yeah, I tried to get out of it, but it's mandatory at this point."

"I can't believe you're still dancin' around with her. Why don't you just end it and put her out of her misery?"

"I just don't have the heart."

"Oh, she's got you on the ropes, doesn't she? Sounds to me like you're goin' down, pal."

"No way! Not me, man! I'm not goin' down. I'm never goin' down."

"Yeah, sure."

"I'm serious."

This kind of talk inspired some wacky improvisations. That night at the Mandarin, I excused myself politely for a quick trip to the men's room. When I came back, I had my cheeks stuffed with wadded-up toilet paper, and launched into an impromptu imitation of Brando's Don Corleone, saying to Jerry, "Don't forget, Michael, whoever comes to you with the Kung Pao Shrimp, he's the traitor! You'll know him by his shrimp."

As usual, Jerry egged me on, gesturing over his plate with his chopsticks and putting on his best Italian accent to ask, "Tell me, Godfather, is the Moo Shoo Pork safe to eat?"

We kept up this relentless running dialogue until our dates began to question our sanity. Karen was always a good sport, and I admired her for being so down-to-earth. I thought she resembled Jerry in a way, with her dark, wavy hair and the shape of her face. They even wore the same style glasses with silver rims. Karen was pre-law and had her own plans for the future. She seemed to look at Jerry's clowning with the boys and his growing interest in the theater as a temporary phase he was going through, something he would grow out of in a year or two.

A week or so later Jerry auditioned for *One Flew Over the Cuckoo's Nest* and landed the part of Martini, the role played by Danny DeVito in the movie. I gave Jerry several pep talks in the student union coffee shop, the Rathskeller, and ran lines with him in my basement for hours. He was already obsessed with performing. But that was the way he was about everything in life, even down to brushing and flossing after every meal—this was a guy who could take an hour to decide what shirt to wear before we went out. He was a fanatic at heart, and so I wasn't really surprised when he caught the acting bug like he did. Everything for Jerry was a performance just waiting for an audience.

The show was a hit, and Jerry got his share of laughs in the small campus theater, King Hall, which only seated about a hundred people. This was a very cozy space, and Jerry did some mugging and invented bits for himself. Jesse Michnick and I were there to lend support on opening night. We were in hysterics watching Jerry ham it up, along with another of our friends, Joey Bacino, who played the part of McMurphy.

Afterwards, Jesse and I went into the dressing room and told Jerry how funny his performance was, especially since this was his first time in front of an audience. We gave him slaps on the back and a few well-chosen compliments. But we couldn't resist razzing him as well. This was expected because nobody in our little gang ever gave anyone the chance to get a swelled head.

Jerry was a senior, and had no idea what he was going to do with his life after graduation. Or so we thought, until the show closed and we all got together for a party at Joey Bacino's house. Joey was a mustachioed, second-generation Italian kid who spoke the language fluently. When I was growing up, he was the one who knew all the curse words and therefore commanded a certain awed respect. Now, like the rest of us, he loved the theater as much as having a good time and that qualified him as a member of our crew. In his case, I was the matchmaker, setting him up with Jesse and Jerry, inadvertently striking an ethnic balance.

Joey lived in Glendale in a house that fit the stereotypical image of the Italian home in the city, at least to the extent that the stereotypes I grew up with sometimes held some grains of truth. His parents kept the rooms on the upper floors immaculate like they were meant to be untouched, with plastic covers over the furniture, and the whole place was decorated with all the meticulous solemnity of a mausoleum. Living was an activity confined exclusively to the basement, where there was a full kitchen, full bath, paneled walls, and hidden fluorescent lighting that glared from the recesses of a dropped ceiling.

It felt like we were making a stage entrance that night when Joey turned on the basement lights for us, and Jerry and Jesse and I came in through the steel double doors. With the end of classes approaching, we were especially buoyant, full of attitude and high spirits. Jerry and I had picked up Jesse and some beer on the way over. We were ready for anything and just sat around talking for a while.

I mentioned in passing that Jerry was the only one of us who hadn't had the pleasure of taking out one of Jesse's very friendly ex-girlfriends, one of those who rightly or wrongly had acquired a reputation for giving away her charms without putting up much of a fight. Jerry caught the drift instantly, saying, "Yeah, and your doctors advised me against seeing her!"

I said to the others, "What do you think—could he keep up with her?"

Joey, who tried to be the authority on these deeply masculine matters, said, "The question is—can Seinfeld keep it up?"

We all snickered rudely, and Jerry's face turned cherry red as he tried to laugh along.

The girl in question had a disturbing laugh and a voice like Gilda Radner's Rosanne Rosannadanna character on *Saturday Night Live*, which was the next topic of conversation, with each of us trying to outdo the others mimicking Steve Martin's "wild and crazy guy." This was all pretty juvenile, frivolous bantering until Jerry leaned forward in his chair, saying, "Listen, I gotta tell you guys something. I'm thinking of doing some comedy."

31

"Comedy?" I said. "Are you serious?"

"Yeah," said Jerry. "I've been thinking about it for a while. It's what I really want to do with my life now. I just didn't want to say anything until I had some material."

We had taken those drama classes together, and over the years I had come to know Jerry's habit of scribbling things down at odd moments on scraps of paper—which told me that he was serious about collecting his thoughts, for whatever reason. Still, I was skeptical and asked Jerry, "You've got material?"

"Yeah, I got material," said Jerry.

I taunted him loudly, "Well, let's hear it, funny boy!"

At that, Jerry stood up and delivered his first monologue, on society's cruel discrimination against left-handed people, from the Bill of Rights to the phrase, "Right on!" He continued this little act with a series of did-ya-ever-notice observations: "Left-handed is so negative, right? Where'd everybody go? They left. And what about having two left feet? Who likes leftovers anyway? I mean, has there ever been a good guy named Lefty?"

His routine was short, and there were a few awkward moments, but at the end, we all roared with laughter. I was impressed with his audacity as much as his jokes. After he sat down, I challenged him to write enough material to fill five minutes, so he could try himself out on amateur night at one of the Manhattan comedy clubs.

I asked him, "What have you got to lose, right?"

The other guys seconded my motion and pumped up his ego, and Jerry quickly said he would try. It didn't taken much to convince him.

The following weekend was Jerry's graduation, and on Monday afternoon I drove him into the City in my car so he could sign up at Catch A Rising Star, one of the clubs that all of us had heard about but had never been to. This was 1976, and the comedy club circuit was booming, but it wasn't a scene where any of us would have gone for our nights on the town.

I helped him rehearse in the car, making suggestions as he made last-minute changes in the routine. He had scripted pieces that seemed to zero in on some of the oddball and offbeat aspects of driving, and going to the beach, and dealing with parents, and shopping; he also worked up a more polished rendition of his left-handed bit. As I listened to him, a lot of this material sounded familiar to me, with lines I'd heard him deliver in conversations between us at one time or another when I had been horsing around, egging him on. Jerry was just being himself, and his routines made me feel like I was somehow being drawn into his stage act, sharing in the sheer fun of it.

That night Jerry and I showed up early at the club, having signed on during the afternoon and spent a few hours waiting in a coffee shop. He had all his notes written on a yellow legal pad. We retreated to the back of the club where Jerry quietly fretted over his script; his nerves and fidgeting made the table wobble between us. He said he wanted to get on and get off. I was amused because he had chosen to be the first onstage, not wanting to give himself the chance to panic while other comics made fools of themselves before him.

Catch A Rising Star was the most popular comedy club in the City at the time, packing in sizable crowds and showcasing many of the best-known comics, along with the unknowns, some of whom would make it big while most would remain unknown forever. Elayne Boosler was the emcee that night. I hurried into the audience and found a seat just as she was introducing Jerry. He took the mike near the front of the stage and just stood there for several long, silent moments, hesitating and squinting out at the crowd until he finally found his voice.

He'd frozen before the first word ever came out of his mouth. I'd never before seen the expression that took control of his face. Like the deer suddenly caught in headlights, this was pure, gawking terror. I still had most of my hair back then, and it was standing on end just watching him. He forgot so many lines that his routine sounded like one non sequitur after another. He jumped from bit to bit without so much as a brief pause or the slightest hint that he was changing the subject. I felt almost as embarrassed for him as he was for himself.

33

When he handed back the mike to Elayne Boosler, she quipped, "That was Jerry Seinfeld, king of segues..."

Afterwards, Jerry was too anguished to even speak. There had been no applause, no laughs except for a few self-conscious guffaws from me. I could see he was devastated, and we didn't hang around to catch the other acts.

As we left the club, I tossed an arm over Jerry's shoulder and told him, "You've got one pair of super *cajones*, my friend. You'll get 'em next time."

"Yeah, sure," said Jerry, still sounding completely downcast. "It's one thing to do it for your friends...but it's another thing to do it for a crowd of strangers who are drinking and talking and couldn't care less about you when you go up on the stage and make an ass of yourself."

As we crossed the street, I tried to cheer him up. Playing with my voice, I said, "Comedy is very dangerous. Very dangerous. Yeah, sure, many times I had to be escorted outta the club...many times..."

We always found a way to laugh.

Chapter Three

The Circuit

Jerry wasn't disheartened or deterred by the setback of his debut. The next week, again on Monday, I drove him back into the City, this time hitting a little piano bar in the Broadway theater district, The Golden Lion, where the management would pull aside a few tables after nine o'clock to make room for a parade of stand-up comics who usually performed for small crowds and no money. Jerry auditioned for the owner that afternoon, with me sitting at a table as lone patron. The Golden Lion offered a more intimate atmosphere than Catch A Rising Star; however, the steady glare from a row of lightbulbs hanging from the ceiling in front of the comic's face made the tiny stage feel like "an interrogation room," as Jerry described it. He called the lights themselves "my french fry lamps."

This was where he got his first taste of truly spontaneous laughter during his act. The place was almost empty when he went on, and there was nothing momentous that night, just a few titters and giggles out in the darkness. But once he had those, there was no turning back. I clapped and hooted after he stepped down, but nothing was more important than the laughter coming from those strangers.

The club circuit quickly became a ritual, with me acting as designated driver because Jerry's nerves made him an unacceptable risk behind the wheel—he was a frantic basket case on a suicide mission. Whichever car we drove, I called the driver's seat and Jerry rode shotgun. While on the road, he would thumb through yellow notepads, soliciting suggestions line by line; then he'd scribble away like mad and make revisions until the last possible moment. On the way, we often picked up Karen and Jesse or others from the old college gang to pack the audience and serve as an enthusiastic cheering section.

What started as a weekly adventure soon took over our lives, with both of us commuting to the City almost every day. Starting at two in the afternoon, we waited on line for Jerry to sign up at Catch a Rising Star or one of the other clubs. We spent hours just pacing the sidewalk or sitting on the curb. If he was lucky enough to get a spot, then we waited again, usually until sometime between eleven and the wee hours of morning when he went onstage. Finally, after catching the last act in the club, we would stop in a coffee shop and unwind before making the drive home, trading stories and gabbing with a cluster of comics and various show biz characters, most of whom were late-night regulars like us.

Jerry played most of the clubs in the City during this period, including The Improv, The Comic Strip, Dangerfield's, Garvin's, The Cellar, and The Bottom Line. Comics were ranked according to their celebrity and seniority. There were some older pros on the circuit like Rodney Dangerfield, Jackie Mason, George Carlin, David Brenner, Robert Klein, and David Steinberg. And there were veterans who had already established themselves like Steve Martin, Tom Hanks, Andy Kaufman, Robin Williams, Sandra Bernhard, Elayne Boosler, Richard Lewis, Jay Leno, David Letterman, Al Franken, George Wallace, and Richard Belzer. Elite status was bestowed on those who appeared on national television or landed a coveted guest spot on Johnny Carson's *Tonight Show*. Jerry was one of a group of talented newcomers that included Paul Reiser, Larry Miller, Carol Leifer, Roseanne Barr, Barry Diamond, and Jimmy Brogan. Watching comics of such caliber night after night was like a crash course for Jerry. The circuit was a cutthroat competition, but for the most part, he remained unfazed—as humble as he was ambitious.

There was a pecking order that determined what spot in the show each comic would have. Prime spots were those later in the evening when the featured comedians would perform for an audience that was warmed up but not yet laughed out. The ultimate kiss of death was to have to go onstage after one of the stars. This was the original meaning of "shrinkage." Jerry occasionally suffered this fate like everyone else, and he would suddenly find himself reliving the nightmare of his first night at Catch A Rising Star. Whenever he died onstage, we joked about the peculiar streak of masochism that drove him to torture his ego this way.

I remember one night we started out by taking in a show at Catch A Rising Star, which was at First Avenue and Seventy-Eighth Street, a few blocks from The Comic Strip where Jerry had booked a later spot. At Catch, we stationed ourselves at a front row table and watched the bizarre routine of Lenny Schultz. Lenny worked as a high school gym teacher in his real life, moonlighting in the clubs at night with a manic, oddball style of humor all his own.

The club was packed that night with a date crowd, mostly in their 20's and 30's, and well-dressed like they had just wandered over from some *Saturday Night Fever* disco scene. The emcee was an enormous fellow with a scratchy voice and baggy suit. He prepared the audience for a rowdy time, with his mike turned all the way up, saying, "I have to warn you, folks, the comic that I'm now going to introduce is actually fu**ing crazy...and I understand he's feeling totally fu**ing insane tonight. So, to keep him in the right mood, when he comes out here, I want you to tell him to GO-FU**ING-CRAZY. Ya got that? Now let's give a big round of applause and hu-u-uge Catch A Rising Star welcome for Crazy Lenny Schultz! Come on out here, Lenny!"

Crazy Lenny charged onto the stage like an epileptic chicken. He was tall and burly, and he did appear deranged with a distorted Afro and his tongue flickering like a lizard's. Jerry was already cracking up and shaking his head in disbelief when Lenny shot past our table. The audience was going wild around us, and I jumped to my feet, knocking over my chair behind me and sending it crashing. I yelled, "Lenny! Go fu**ing crazy!"

With the clamor of my chair, the place suddenly went

silent. Every head in the room turned toward me and then back to the stage to see what Crazy Lenny's reaction would be. Jerry looked on with his eyebrows raised like he had just been hit on the forehead by a pair of darts. Flashing a huge grin, Crazy Lenny bellowed at me, "You-u-u...I like!"

The audience went wild again, and for the rest of the night Jerry and I kept repeating, "You-u-u...I like!"

Such was the anything-goes atmosphere where Jerry tested his material. His act was very tame compared to what some of his peers were foisting on audiences. But Jerry was never tempted to include obscenities or any jokes that might be considered crude or vulgar. Nor was he into shock comedy.

After Lenny finished his act, we walked to The Comic Strip, which was even more crowded. A velvet rope cordoned off the line waiting to get in. We slipped through to the bar where there was an unofficial fashion show in progress, the hip and beautiful showing off the latest in nightclub chic. "A little glitter goes a long way," shouted Jerry into my ear, his voice all but drowned out by the sound system, which was blasting Bruce Springsteen's, "Prove It All Night."

This was a typical scene. We could see the stage through the thick, soundproof window at the end of the bar. There was no hope of ordering a drink; the bar was backed up three-deep, and the two of us just stood paralyzed, scanning some of the pretty faces on the make. Jerry was in jeans, a checkered sports shirt, and sneakers. This was his uniform, versatile enough to fit any occasion.

I asked, "When do you go on?"

He said, "I think I'm after Ed Bluestone."

"You should kill in that spot," I told him.

"I don't know," he said. "Bluestone's got a pretty good act. Did you hear his line about Jewish hunting?"

"No. How's it go?"

"They bring the animals to the house tied up in a cage."

We both laughed, practically wrapped up in each other's arms, succumbing to claustrophobia. I asked over the din, "Why don't you do any Jewish jokes? They go over big."

"Too easy," he said, "and boring. It's the same shtick over and over. I have to do what I do, Mike. It has to come from who I am."

"What are you doing tonight?" I asked him. "The Tide?"

"Yeah," he said, referring to one of his earliest jokes that questioned the sanity of commercials boasting Tide detergent could get out bloodstains.

Continuing a third degree interrogation that had started back in the car on the way in, he asked, "You really like how I changed the bumper cars?"

"Yeah," I said. "I told you. It's great."

This was another early bit about the hapless father-and-son team trying to steer a broken bumper car through an amusement park ride. He kept this one in his repertoire on and off for years, and eventually he would use it again for one of his opening monologues on Seinfeld. He was continually changing and reworking his jokes, trying to keep them fresh. Yet he was beset at times by bouts of absent-mindedness worthy of a nutty professor.

At about that point in the evening, we were approached by a couple of attractive coeds from Queens, and one of them said she recognized Jerry. "I saw your show—really great! How do you remember all that stuff?" It was the line of lines. Jerry gave her a killer smile, then gave me an eye roll. The coed, whoever she may have been, was one of the first to ask for his autograph. Jerry was flattered and signed one of The Comic Strip placemat menus. He also accepted her phone number although, as soon as she was gone, he tossed it—he was still seeing Karen, and was never much interested in the rough-and-tumble of chance encounters.

Jerry made it through his act that night without forgetting too many of his lines. This was still something of a problem for him. From my table, I yelled out the names of bits that he hadn't done yet—like the bumper cars—which somehow had slipped his mind. At the end of the act, he turned to me from the stage and asked, "Have I left anything else out?"

I waved him off, and Jerry made his exit. There was only a

polite smattering of applause. Moments later he explained to me, "The audience is plotzed. Let's get outta here."

We walked around the corner to a restaurant called the Green Kitchen and congratulated ourselves for having made it through one more night. When we walked in, I passed a rack of computer dating questionnaires and brought one with me to the table. The questions were a personality survey like those you find in glamour magazines that give you some sort of "Romance IQ."

This kind of thing often gave us a laugh or two, and Jerry insisted on going through the questions. He asked, "If you could have one of these in your life, what would it be—Fame? Money? Power? Love? Serenity?" Without giving me a chance to answer, Jerry said, "I'll take serenity."

"Why serenity?" I asked him, thinking that love sounded like a better choice at this hour.

He skipped ahead to the next question. "Here's a good one. Where would you most want to go on your date—To a movie? To a restaurant? To the beach? To your date's house?" He looked up at me from the questionnaire and said, "Yeah, what if we both want to go to each other's houses? We might never even see each other. That'll keep the romance fresh, huh?"

When it was this late, anything might suddenly capture our attention and crack us up. It didn't surprise me to see pieces of our conversations come back later as bits on the stage—that was just the way Jerry worked; every conversation was a search for material.

Like most of the other comics of his generation, Jerry never bought jokes, and he looked with disdain on those who did. He had a personal ethic about comedy that was very instinctual. There was only one time that I disagreed with him, and it involved an episode with Elayne Boosler, who was gaining popularity when Jerry started out. Elayne was fairly aggressive, and she was quite talented with her style of comedy, spoofing gender and sex, even the guy code.

At the time this happened, Jerry had been doing a bit about *Jaws*. In this routine, Jerry suggested that the movie was not all that suspenseful. "We always know when the shark is coming because we hear that cello music. I don't know why people don't just swim back to shore when they hear the music. They should be yelling, OH, NO, CELLO MUSIC. LET'S MAKE A RUN FOR IT!"

Not long after Jerry had first performed the joke at Catch A Rising Star, Elayne, wittingly or unwittingly, incorporated the same joke into her act on a night when she happened to appear on Johnny Carson's *Tonight Show*. When I heard Elayne repeat the bit, almost word for word, I thought that it was a low blow for Jerry. I said to him, "Doesn't it get you mad? I'd be pissed off. I mean, she used your material, didn't she?"

He didn't care. If anything, he was glad she had liked his joke enough to use it in her act. If his bit could get laughs for her from Johnny's audience, Jerry knew that he had to be writing quality material.

When I tried to press him further, he said, "You know, Mikey, all's fair in love and comedy..."

* * *

That summer of 1976, after Jerry's graduation and his launch into the comedy scene, I was secretly wrestling with what I wanted to do with my own life and my future in the theater. I was anxious to break into the real world where the action was— Queens College already seemed like the old days. Our buddy, Jesse, was leaving to take a job with a TV station upstate, so I was the only one of our trio who was still looking forward to returning to classes in the fall.

The three of us made a weekend trip to the Catskills where Jerry's parents owned a vacation cabin overlooking the Villa Roma resort hotel in the town of Callicoon—an Italian section of the Catskills, we soon discovered—the "Bocci Belt" as opposed to the "Borscht Belt," long famous for its legendary, die-hard comics from another era. There were still a few on the circuit, although stars like Henny Youngman and Shecky Green were gone. Not long before we left on our getaway, Jackie Mason had caught

Jerry's act, and Jerry had been thrilled ever since the famous comic complimented him and shook his hand, offering up a few priceless words of encouragement: "Ta tell ya the truth, I look at you and I can see that you're a funny guy—and oooooh, I can't stand ya!"

Though Jerry wasn't really doing Jewish comedy, he still had an ardent respect for the old masters, and Jackie Mason would one day pay his compliments on Jerry's all-embracing comic style in *The New York Times*. In my mind as a young actor, this was like having Marlon Brando say there was hope in this world for you, bestowing his personal blessing on your talent.

After reaching the Seinfeld cabin, the three of us spent an afternoon hiking around and goofing off, taking in the natural beauty with all the enthusiasm of city kids let loose in the wilds. The only squabble on this trip occurred after we decided to turn in that night and realized that there were only two beds for the three of us. Jesse was quick to claim the single in the living room, and Jerry grumbled about having to share the other bed, tossing his barbs my way. He was afraid of being "Costanzarized" in his sleep, and he didn't see how he was going to survive the night. Neither did I, after I saw the mattress was a waterbed.

I asked him, "Seinfeld, what were your parents thinking when they put in the waterbed? They figured you'd bring girls up here for wild orgies, right?"

It was a shaky rite of passage, and I suppose there must be some sort of bond that only two guys in their underwear can forge as friends trying not to breathe or make waves, and then suffering all of those slings and arrows and recriminations the next morning. We walked around complaining of motion sickness. Still, there was a semi-serious moment over cereal when I said that I wasn't going back to school in the fall—that I was going to study acting in the City and get started on my career. My mind was made up, and Jerry voiced approval without making a joke.

After our return, I immersed myself in theater, studying at Stella Adler's method studio, taking classes with Bill Hickey at HB Studio, and Anthony Mannino at the Drama Tree. Jerry always took a very active interest in these pursuits of mine, and I became especially close to Anthony Mannino, who was highly regarded and had been a mentor for Harvey Keitel. When it came to drama, if I learned anything new, Jerry was keen to absorb it.

Our time was now split between the club circuit, the various theater scenes in Manhattan, and the necessity of making a living. In the fall, the two of us worked for a while as unlicensed street peddlers—with Jerry selling little jewelry items on a cart, and me hawking wholesale sweaters from Brooklyn, both of us plying our trade in the area of Bloomingdale's. I staked out a prize spot in front of Arby's that made a mint; Jerry wasn't as lucky with his trinkets. Who buys jewelry from a comedian?

There were occasions when we had to flee the cops, and this sort of thing was a reminder that neither of us had fulfilled our parents' expectations thus far in our lives. The question—what will your parents say?—was usually answered with a shrug of the shoulders, or with some evasive grimace, neither of us wishing to acknowledge that our career choices fell short of their aspirations.

Jerry received an early, unexpected vote of confidence and a career boost after Rodney Dangerfield caught his act one night and signed him for an HBO special that September—*Rodney Dangerfield: It's Not Easy Bein' Me*. The show included sketches for Dangerfield and Roseanne Barr, who was just starting out, as well as a showcase for young comics. Despite the trademark complaint in his act about not getting any, Dangerfield commanded as much respect as any comic on the circuit. Whenever he walked into a club, the crowd would part like the sea; he thrived on his audience, and could read the room at a glance. When we first saw him, Jerry said to me, "It's like he gets his energy just from the buzz."

Dangerfield represented the pantheon of comic gods, and Jerry counted his lucky stars to have caught his eye for the show. After some agonized decision-making about which bits to use, Jerry donned a dark, bell-bottom suit for the occasion and performed a couple of tried-and-true jokes for the cameras. He only had a total of about ten minutes of material in his entire act at this point, so I heard his standard riffs hundreds of times. Bumper cars. The mystery of losing socks in the laundry. The hazardous absurdities of computer dating. It was the audiences that kept the jokes alive, because he never knew on a given night which bits would work with a particular crowd. As soon as there was any laughter, a joke extended its life through one more show. He had a bit about Earth Shoes in the early days that died as soon as the shoe went off the market. This weeding-out process went on for years. The survival of the funniest—Jerry knew this applied to comics as well as to their jokes.

The Dangerfield special didn't lead to any major recognition, but at least Jerry was able to make the case with his parents that his career was showing some promise—suddenly, he was one of the fortunate few who had been on TV. He was also earning thirty-five dollars one night a week as an emcee at The Comic Strip. Although the pay was miserable, being an emcee was an essential rung on the ladder for any comic to become recognized as a featured performer, and he was already on his way.

Jerry was soon asked to play one of the big rooms in the Catskills, and we piled into the back of a van to drive upstate for a one-night show at the Raleigh Hotel. We made this trip with a female comedian, Carol Leifer, a feisty, free-spirited blonde who Jerry described as a "guy's girl." Carol was quick-witted and knew how to hold her own with the boys. Later, she and Jerry would have a short romantic affair. He admitted to me years afterwards that Carol had indeed been an inspiration for the character of Elaine; he even hired her as one of the writers on the show. Of course, Jerry knew quite a few funny women as time went on, and every character on the show became a composite drawn from life.

It is unlikely that Carol fell for him during the Catskills encounter, unless it was out of pity, as Jerry bombed royally that night at the Raleigh. The place was majestic, but his voice was the only sound in the room. When he stepped offstage, I told him, "You might as well have been on the top of Everest." After such a humbling experience, he had the feeling that he was starting all over again, but he took it in stride.

A month or two before Christmas that year, I showed Jerry a newspaper ad for actors to play Santa Claus at Macy's. I figured if nothing else, it was a paying job and the chance to act. There were auditions, and I asked him if he wanted to go with me. Jerry gave me one of his gigantic stage grins, saying facetiously, "You better go ahead without me, Mike. I have to check with my rabbi first."

I loved the job, sitting with two and three-year-olds, trying to get them to smile for the camera by charming them with toys like the Cookie Monster, Jack-in-the-Box, and Oscar the Grouch. One day Jerry stopped by and sat on my lap—which caused quite a stir for the kids on hand. Perched absurdly, he asked, "So, did that Santa job ever come through?" Of course, neither of us ever dreamed while living through this forgettable episode that one day Kramer would also decide to put in a stint as department store Santa at Macy's, though Jerry would leave out the rabbi joke.

In 1974 Jerry and I started a yearly Christmas ritual of seeing the holiday show at Rockefeller Center. We would meet beneath the tree and spend the evening taking in the festivities. Standing in that spot and looking up, as we did many times, annually revealed the towering headquarters of NBC.

Of course, we never dreamed...

* * *

In the spring, Jerry hit me with two startling announcements, one coming on top of the other: he was moving into Manhattan, and his relationship with Karen was over. The second piece of news was a shocker, at least for me, like Superman suddenly breaking up with Lois Lane. But both Karen and Jerry knew that he was going to stay on the club circuit and that she was going to law school. This was reason enough for the split. Their lives were now about to move in entirely different directions, and Jerry was the type of person who wanted everything in his life to have a definite beginning and end, like his act. At this stage, he looked at marriage as an endless date.

Following the code as applied to breakups, I lost touch with Karen once she became the ex-girlfriend. But Jerry managed to stay in contact with her sporadically through the years and maintained their friendship.

The move from his parents' house into the City happened over a weekend with a rented U-haul truck. I met him at the apartment, a four-flight walk-up at 129 West 81st Street and the two of us carried boxes and furniture up to the fourth floor.

This 400-square-foot studio was much more modest than the spacious, one-bedroom apartment that eventually would be used for his set on *Seinfeld*, and Jerry didn't put quite as much energy into fixing up his place as the Hollywood set decorators did. The only windows in his studio offered no views of the street, but looked down onto the rooftop of an adjacent building. Jerry's taste was both minimalist and practical when it came to the furnishings. He had a daybed and a small round table where he usually kept a pile of yellow notepads and enough pens to be sure that he was always ready to set down new ideas, which often came without warning, even in the middle of our conversations. At those times, I would simply stretch out on the daybed and quietly wait for him to finish writing.

To this spartan environment, he also added a couch—one of those bulky, leather monsters with brass grommets around the edges of the arms and base. On the floor next to the couch, Jerry placed a wooden magazine rack that I brought along as an apartment-warming gift. I watched as he methodically unloaded his boxes. One of the charms of the apartment was a fireplace—on its mantle, he placed a change jar where would keep off-the-books earnings from survival jobs. We set a bureau next to the bathroom door, and then he carefully taped up a pair of photographs on the wall above. One was a shot of George Burns; the other featured old-timers Edgar Bergen and Charlie McCarthy. I asked Jerry, "Why them, of all the comics in the world?"

He said, "I want to be in this business as long as these guys. They remind me of what I need to do to have the kind of act that it takes to be that good and have that kind of longevity." He added, "I want to grow old in Las Vegas."

It didn't seem strange to me at all that he was twenty-three years old and already thinking about achieving immortality as a stand-up. I wanted to grow old in Hollywood as an actor, although I planned to keep a place in New York as well. Home was home.

Naturally, there were some practical details that we would have to attend to before allowing ourselves to be swept up in the bright lights of stardom. We ventured out to a nearby mom-and-pop grocery to stock up on essentials. After we unpacked back at the apartment, Jerry stood outside the bathroom door, absorbed by a roll of toilet paper.

He looked up from the package and asked, "What do you think they mean by 'facial quality'? Does that make any sense to you?"

And another bit was born.

The apartment soon became a regular hangout for us and for quite a few comic friends on the circuit, like Larry Miller, Henry Wallace (an ad executive who later reinvented himself in stand-up as George Wallace), Mark Schiff, Carol Leifer and Jimmy Brogan. As I was still living at home with my parents, I sometimes crashed on the couch after late nights in the clubs. Jerry's cozy pad became my home away from home. As depicted on the show, this was the place where we told stories and talked about nothing in particular at great length.

Forbidden Meatballs

One of the early stories I remember telling Jerry involved my forcible ejection from a movie theater in Forest Hills. I had gone alone to catch a matinee of Woody Allen's *Annie Hall*. Before going into the movie, I picked up a meatball sandwich from a new pizzeria that had opened by the theater. This was all innocent enough until the ushers and manager asked me to leave, as "foreign food" was not allowed into the movie house.

I refused to exit and hunkered down in the darkness watching the flick, loving Woody and happily fantasizing about Diane

Keaton until a flashlight-wielding SWAT team descended upon me. By now I had eaten my sandwich, but one police officer spotted the telltale signs of meatballs and tomato sauce on the front of my shirt; so I was escorted out by a dozen men in blue.

I railed against the Gestapo policies of the theater, and pointed out for Jerry that more cops had been sent to pick me up than they sent to nab Lee Harvey Oswald in that Dallas movie house. Jerry absorbed the tale like a comic sponge, and years later passed it off to Kramer—who was unceremoniously ejected from a *Seinfeld* movie theater for bringing in an illicit *caffè latte*. Thanks to Jerry, the fictional Kramer would take the absurd situation one step further by filing a suit against the coffee shop chain after being scalded by his coffee.

A lawsuit. I wish I'd thought of that.

The Pole Lock

This was not a Polish joke, but the story of a pole lock. Jerry proved himself to be the champion storyteller, but he was also the best straight man around. Many times he would come out with punch lines that were simply a part of his personality, his peculiar way of twisting the world to suit his needs, especially inside his apartment where he was like a probing detective. He played this role on one occasion after he'd been burgled several times in a period of weeks, with thieves making off with the TV and stereo, then coming back to snatch the replacements.

After the burglaries, Jerry had the super put a new lock on the door, one of those heavy dead bolts, figuring this was sure to keep the culprits out. But a week later, he came home to find that thieves had blown a small hole in the wall by the door, reached in to unlock the door, then helped themselves once again. Jerry subsequently shopped around the city for the best lock he could find. Whenever he shopped for anything, he had a way of making a federal case out of it, first researching *Consumer Reports*, then bombarding salespeople with questions for hours on end, like an amateur Ralph Nader.

After doing his usual thorough job with locks and locksmiths, Jerry came home with the pole, known as a "police lock." This was a heavy iron rod that fit between the door handle and a hole in the floor, essentially jamming the door shut to any would-be intruders. Jesse and I found Jerry the next afternoon, after he had installed the new device. He recounted the entire saga for us, blow-by-blow, and he had us entranced, winning our sympathies as he lamented his run of bad luck, with the three of us huddled by the door.

Jerry said, "I couldn't believe it! They blew a hole right through the wall."

Jesse asked with genuine interest, "But, Jerry, didn't your neighbors complain about the noise?"

Jerry fumed, "Yeah—when I was fixing it!"

A typical *Seinfeld* moment.

He had the last laugh as always, as the burglars never got past the invincible pole. It was one possession Jerry took great pride in, though it proved to be too realistic a detail for the *Seinfeld* set.

Lightbulbs

Jobs were always a sore topic for us. Jerry vowed never to take a serious job that he couldn't leave at a moment's notice to pursue his real career. He saw dead-end jobs as a way to motivate himself, if only out of desperation. He kept himself in the throes of extreme poverty—most of the time he was barely able to afford socks, or a box of Tide. As far as making ends meet, I was usually more resourceful than Jerry was. I had a hack license to fall back on, having worked as a cabbie since the age of 19. It was me who bragged to Jerry that I could make the drive from his place on West 81st to Kennedy in fifteen minutes; and so it happened that I passed on my driving skills (and secret knowledge of shortcuts through Queens) to George.

Jerry and I were always seeking out new employment. He set us up with a part-time sales position through a contact that he had downtown, a small-time hustler named Al Fass. All that Jerry could tell me about the job was that it involved selling long-life lightbulbs over the phone. I was doubtful at first, but one afternoon the two of us went downtown and visited the General Lightsearch Company on Nineteenth Street off Fifth Avenue. Once inside the offices, we were greeted by Al Fass himself, a hyper, fast-talking character in a striped business suit.

Al told us, "You guys are just in time. I've only got two desks left. Let me show you around. Follow me. Right this way, boys. You're gonna love the job. It's a great deal for actors. You can make your own hours here."

He led us into the back room, a warren of tacky cubicles and tiny offices with desks and telephones. As we passed through, Al gave an enthusiastic thumbs-up sign to the members of his sales crew, all ages and types. The place sounded like a cocktail party with fifty conversations going at once—a boiler room operation, with everybody talking into phones, making pitches that were read from scripts.

Al showed us to adjoining cubicles and welcomed us aboard, saying, "You guys will need to change your names." After a quick consultation, I dubbed myself "Mike Davis," and Jerry became "Dave Wilson." Al outfitted us with telephone books, and the company's sales scripts, with which we were expected to dupe unsuspecting lightbulb buyers all over the country.

Two cases of bulbs went for just under four hundred dollars, and we pocketed eighty as commission. So each of us tried to sell at least four cases a day, putting in a few hours in the office and then taking off for more lofty pursuits. The problem was that the scripts were lame and deadly boring. So we wrote our own back at Jerry's apartment, or we improvised.

Jerry had just started working with an improv group, and he showed a certain flair and knack for thinking on his feet when he applied his talents to selling bulbs. Sometimes we fell far below the standards of taste and decency that Jerry normally exhibited in his act. I would say, "Hello. This is Mike Davis. You remember me? The handicapped veteran? We spoke a little while ago, and you ordered two cases of lightbulbs from me." With Jerry looking on from his cubicle, I would drop the phone and knock it around. "Sorry, it's hard to get used to these hooks. Listen, I'm going to send you a bonus set of carving knives...if you'll just confirm your order with me today..."

By the time I hung up, we would be on the floor laughing and giggling like a pair of bad schoolboys—this was before the days of politically correct enlightenment, and also before either of us had personal experience with the handicapped. Recalling the scene reminds me how we matured in spite of ourselves, and how the years ahead would change us in so many unforeseen ways.

We were at Jerry's apartment a short time later when our boss, Al Fass, telephoned to say there was no need for us to come back to work. The police had turned the lights out in the boiler room, and the General Lightsearch Company had already moved across the river to New Jersey.

Looking back on our lightbulb experience years later, Jerry would summarize it perfectly, "Tough job. There aren't many people sitting at home saying, I'M HERE IN THE DARK. I CAN'T HOLD OUT MUCH LONGER!"

After the bulbs, Jerry went on to work at a Brew and Burger, saving tips for cab fare until he got his second night as emcee at The Comic Strip. He was making about seventy bucks a week at this point, and figured he was golden. A full-time, paid entertainer.

War Stories

There was always another tale to tell around the fireplace whenever we came back from the road. Scrapes with club managers. Lunatic hecklers. Unnatural disasters. Near seductions by *femmes fatales*. Bizarre bloopers. Hostile audiences. In Princeton, New Jersey, a group of college students went slightly berserk at a frat party, and the show turned out to be a little like telling jokes to a group of Hell's Angels. A true *Animal House* nightmare, with the decibel level of the band driving Jerry to despair and bottles of beer sailing by our heads. I appointed myself bodyguard for the evening, as Jerry-the-trooper insisted on our sticking it out.

For a couple of years, we made frequent trips to another of the Catskill resort venues, the Brickman, where all of the comics who were working the upstate circuit would gather one night a week for a private party. The show was for established comics only, who played to each other, and such a great learning experience was far too tempting to pass up. The first time we went, Jesse led the way by cleverly impersonating the owner of the Bottom Line, Paul Colby, ushering us past hotel security so we could crash the festivities and take in the likes of Eddie Shaefer, the venerable emcee, and comedians Sal Richard and Freddy Roman.

At the time, Jesse was working up in Watertown and was able to arrange a special gig for Jerry at a local club, coincidentally named The Golden Lion. The plan called for Jerry and me to take one of those tiny, fly-by-night airlines; the plane was no larger than Jerry's apartment, and the last leg of the journey turned out to be hair-raising, like the flight of the bumblebee. We were teetering and still white-knuckled after we landed at the Watertown airport where Jesse picked us up and then chauffeured us straight to the club.

So we weren't in the best of moods, and Jerry quickly had to deal with an interview by a local TV personality, Jeff Grahan, the future mayor of the town. Jerry was low-key until he went onstage and checked out the audience. This was a case of the city slicker meeting his match, with many in the crowd wearing cowboy boots, ear muffs and winter gear, somehow giving the impression that they were waiting for a country-and-western jamboree.

Jerry's opening line set the tone for the night. "How many people up here know what a joke is? Raise your hands."

It went downhill from there. The socks. Nothing. The gag where he mocked the way smokers used their cigarettes to punctuate their sentences. Nothing. I figured maybe it was a smoking crowd. The computer dating stuff? More nothing. Bumper cars? Forget it. He was heckled by some smart-ass and Jerry pulled out one of his less artful put-down lines, asking the guy, "Aren't your parents first cousins?"

We were lucky to get out alive. This was not the sort of show that inspired great faith in the future. During the flight back to the Big Apple, Jerry confided that he was thinking about taking on a personal manager. I thought he might be joking, and kidded him, waving my pen in front of our two faces like a cigar, saying, "You're gonna be big one day, kid, and I mean really big. You're goin' to the top! Stick with me, and you'll have twenty-four carrots instead of diamonds."

Jerry just looked at me the way Abbott would have looked at Costello.

* * *

There was a support balance between us, with me serving as Jerry's sidekick on the circuit, and with him coming to workshops and plays that I did off-off-Broadway. He attended my graduation from the Drama Tree during the summer of 1978 when I performed the role of Bickham (originated by Al Pacino) in the play, *Does A Tiger Wear a Necktie*? After the show, we went out for pizza at our usual stop on Columbus Avenue, Tom's Pizza (the actual place that *Seinfeld*'s Monk's Restaurant tried to duplicate), a few blocks up from Jerry's place. In the midst of our usual pizza banter, Jerry handed me a plastic tiger with a tiny homemade tie wrapped around its neck. After making the gesture, he said, "Now what, Costanza?"

I knew what he meant. I said, "I'll hit the pavement again. Go to some cattle calls. An agent saw me tonight. So who knows? He asked me to come see him."

Jerry said, "Comedians aren't like actors. We have a place to go to work every night. Comics don't mind being amateurs, at least for a while, starting out. I don't know any actor, even in a student play, who would ever admit to being an amateur."

I chuckled and said, "Yeah, right. Maybe I'll do a monologue standing in front of the Schubert Theater."

"With the jugglers!" said Jerry. "They seem to do all right.

I don't know any starving jugglers. It must not take all that much to juggle your way to the top."

There was an edge under our laughter whenever the real world reared its ominous head. Still, the magnetic realm was comedy and Jerry was moving as fast as he could. He made paying his dues into a joyride, even when the hecklers or an oblivious audience marred his act on a given night.

During our late-night stints at the Green Kitchen and back in his apartment, Jerry was conducting a sort of joke school. He had already won the respect of his peers and some would ask advice or consult him about their routines. He was generous, trying to help even the most hopeless cases. Jerry was smart enough to avoid the pitfalls of alcohol and drugs that he saw ruin acts. A few comics were notorious: Freddie Prinz and John Belushi who took their self-destructive impulses to the extreme. But there were others we knew pretty well, and there were nights we'd see them, glassy-eyed and trying to tell us they had just killed onstage—when we knew there hadn't been a laugh in the house. Jerry was a control freak in some ways, and to embarrass himself in that fashion wasn't ever a remote possibility. Not that he didn't love having fun. But he was more likely to enjoy an intellectual evening at a party thrown by Robert Klein, than waste his time the way some of his crazier cohorts did.

Jerry had two things that kept him on the straight and narrow most of the time: one was his absolute devotion to stand-up; the other was his own self-styled spiritual discipline, which went back to meditation and yoga. At the time, there was a Scientology center near his apartment, and he took some classes and read books by L. Ron Hubbard. But Jerry never went overboard with any of the mystical cult stuff or personal gurus, and he knew better than to try to encourage me.

Jerry took what he needed to perform and found whatever other answers he needed to please himself—whether it was Zen, or going with me to the U.S. Open Tennis tournament, which became another of our yearly thrills. Thanks to one of Jesse's connections, we often got tickets to the tournament although these were never great seats. Jerry and I became experts at choosing just the right moment in the match to move from our cheap seats to the front rows, where we were usually able to insinuate ourselves for the rest of the tournament. All was fair in love and comedy—and tennis.

The Fat Man and Robert DeNiro

I remember charging up the four flights of stairs to Jerry's apartment in the winter of 1979 to deliver the news about my latest audition and career setback. This little side show had started two months before when I received a call from Uncle Sal, or rather, a summons that he wanted to see me.

I hadn't heard from him in several years, not since the last time he had gone away on "vacation." I went over to his villa pronto, and Uncle Sal received me in his basement, wearing a smoking jacket and sitting in front of his fireplace. It was like a scene out of a bad movie. The coiffed mane of silver hair. The diamond pinky ring. He was even stroking his German shepherd as I walked in. "Michael," he said. "C'mere. We have to talk."

He got up to his feet and kissed my cheek. When we sat down, he asked, "Tell me, how are your brothers?"

I told him my brothers were fine, and it was good to have him back. Uncle Sal thanked me for looking after his son while he was away, adding that he'd been told I had done the right thing by him. Then he asked me, "You still trying to be the actor?"

"I'm still acting," I told him.

He handed me a card with a name on it and said, "Call this guy. He's a friend of mine. Just mention my name."

Uncle Sal made small talk for a few minutes, and then made it clear it was time for me to leave.

The following week I followed his instructions to the letter, and suddenly, I had an appointment to see a man named Irwin Schiff, who was actually a partner in a reputable talent agency. I visited him in his midtown office. He was sitting behind a white lacquered desk and looked like he weighed almost four hundred pounds—one of the fattest men I had ever seen. I gave him my picture and resume, and he asked me about myself for a few minutes, putting me at ease. After he had what he needed from me, he leaned forward and winked, saying quietly, "Let me see what I can do, Michael. I'll be in touch with you."

I didn't expect anything to come of it, but I was impressed with Irwin Schiff. True to his word, he called some weeks later. He asked if I knew how to box and, like any actor hungry for work, I exaggerated my abilities to see what kind of role he might have in mind for me. He said, "How'd you like to meet Robert DeNiro? I've got an audition for you."

I was beside myself after we hung up—not only with the possibility of getting an acting job, but also with the prospect of meeting one of my all-time idols.

The following day I went into the posh Paramount offices in Manhattan and met the casting director, Cis Corman, who showed me into a small conference room where DeNiro himself was seated. Cis made the introduction. I said the first thing that came to mind, "My mother said I should bring you home for dinner, because you're so skinny." DeNiro laughed good-naturedly and then looked over my resume, making some comments about my training and the teachers he knew. Obviously, he was far more relaxed than I was. A real gentleman. He coached me for the part, and I did my best with a short reading. After I finished, we thanked each other and shook hands again.

That was it. I had just auditioned for a new movie called *Raging Bull* though I didn't know it at the time, and I waited anxiously through the week to hear back on it. I was still waiting when I went out one morning and saw the front pages of the newspapers featuring Irwin Schiff's picture. He was lying in a pool of blood in front of an Italian restaurant. It was alleged in the news articles that he had ties to the mob. That was the news I carried with me when I ran up those four flights of stairs to Jerry's apartment. This was one way of losing out on a role that I had never imagined. My agent was dead.

Jerry already knew. He just shook his head and said,

"Mikey, you've done it again."

* * *

In 1980, after putting in four years on the New York circuit, Jerry decided he was ready to make the move to L.A. It was natural. One of his longtime pals, Jimmy Brogan, had gone out there the year before. This was an inevitable leap for those comics who wanted to play to a different club crowd and try their luck at breaking into television. Jerry had signed with Spotlight, a management agency that handled only comics, and they encouraged him.

A group of us went to a going-away party for Jerry held at McSorley's Pub, which was the oldest bar in New York City and had only recently changed a century-old policy of not allowing females to enter. There were no women in our little party of well-wishers that night. The group included Jesse and me, Larry Miller, George Wallace, Chris Misiano, and another young comic, Dennis Wolfburg. Between the six of us and the bartender, we succeeded in giving Jerry a raucous, bon voyage roasting.

At the end of the night, I dropped Jerry back at his place. This was one of the very few times I remember him having had more than a couple beers. We were still joking around, acting out some of the sentimental lines from Casablanca—I don't recall which of us was supposed to be Humphrey Bogart and which was Ingrid Bergman. I could tell he was psyched about the move, and his excitement was no doubt mixed up with some fear of the unknown. I was happy for him but, at the same time, I knew that I was going to miss the guy.

After we hugged and Jerry laughed his way into the building, I stood outside on the sidewalk, wondering to myself...now what, Costanza?

I knew he'd be back. New York was his home too. But it was one of those moments in my life when I knew things would never be quite the same.

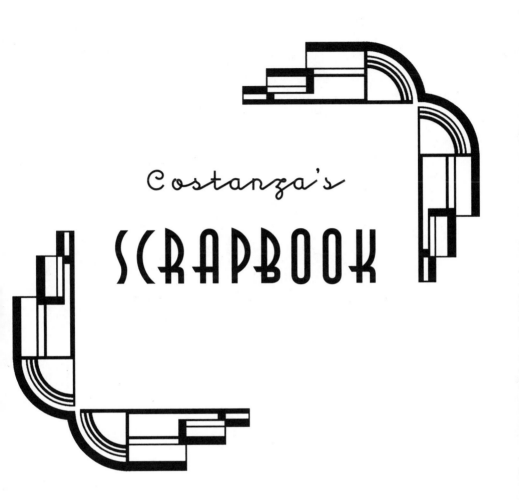

Costanza's
SCRAPBOOK

Jerry when I first met him in '74.

My folks' house in Queens where we hung out.

The Real Costanzas—Joe and Millie—my mother and father.

61

Queens College - Kings Hall.

Flyer for Jerry's disastrous gig in Watertown.

The Comic Strip.

The Green Kitchen, our late-night hangout, was down the block from
Catch a Rising Star.

Jerry and me in my apartment in '81.

Jerry and Joe Bacino in my apartment in Queens.

Jesse's wedding in '82.

The old gang got together to celebrate Jerry's first spot on the Johnny Carson show.

The old gang celebrating my 31st birthday on a yacht in '86——me, Joey, Jerry and Jesse.

Jerry, Jesse, Gary and me at the party.

Costanza and Costanza—need I say more?

Me and Wayne Knight ("Newman") on the back lot '92.

Reunion with Michael—he opened for Jerry at Carnegie Hall.

I'm wearing my rug with the Queens College "rat pack" at Carnegie Hall in '92.

Chapter Four

The Breaks

Jerry kept his apartment on West 81st Street. He looked at his stay in L.A. as being "on the road." At times, I was tempted to follow him to pursue my acting career in Hollywood, but his reports of La La Land on the phone were filled with bleak, gallows humor—I knew that he was hurting out there. He said he was going through "New York withdrawal." Just a few months later he came home for a quick visit and went into hiding at home with his parents out on Long Island, until I lured him into town.

We spent one night romping through familiar club haunts, and I listened to Jerry's tales of rejection at TV casting calls—he accepted these setbacks less easily than any of the bad nights he'd ever had onstage. He told me about his new life on the L.A. circuit, working, struggling, improvising. He'd rented a small apartment in West Hollywood in the same building where his comedian ally, Jimmy Brogan, had been living. But Jerry wasn't ever going to adjust to exile. He was carrying too much baggage along with him—all of the typical New York prejudices against the superficialities and absurdities of life on the west coast.

There were other reasons I wasn't inclined to head west at this point. For one, my family needed me. My mother had passed away with cancer the year before and, like my father and brothers, I was still pretty broken up about it. Jerry had made the trip to Queens to come to the wake and offer his support. Over the years, we joked about a lot of things, but some parts of life were sacred without our ever needing to say so. Jerry was there for me. It was the first time that he had ever seen tears in my eyes that hadn't been caused by laughter.

At the wake, I introduced Jerry to my new girlfriend, Marie Hollins, whom I had only recently met. Marie was from Queens like me and, as I told Jerry later, she was "GD"—our abbreviation for geographically desirable. After Jerry went back to Los Angeles, he would ask about her during our phone calls. He could sense that it was going to be something serious for me and the outlandish idea that I might be the first from the old crew to go down the aisle caused him perverse delight. He needled me mercilessly.

Meeting Marie was one of those strange, star-crossed events which, up until this point in my life, I thought happened only in movies. At the time, Marie was a dental assistant. She worked in the Park Avenue office of Dr. Michael Uris. It so happened that one of Dr. Uris's patients was an actor named Jerry Stiller, who was known for his part in the husband-and-wife comedy team of Stiller and Meara (with wife Anne Meara). In the 60's, they had been regulars on the Ed Sullivan Show and they were among the early stand-up acts that had captivated Jerry in his tender youth.

Even my father and I had watched Stiller and Meara, and my father often heckled Stiller in jest, speaking aloud to our old black-and-white TV. As a dental patient, Jerry Stiller befriended Marie and gave her tickets for a Broadway show in which he was appearing, *The Ritz*. Imagine my amazement when I learned more than ten years later that Jerry Stiller had been cast on *Seinfeld* to play the role of Frank Costanza—George's father!—and purely by coincidence, if you're the kind of person who believes in coincidence. It was as if my pal of pals, Jerry Seinfeld, was destined to become the jokester magician holding up a mirror to my life and to all the lives that mine happened to touch.

Destiny was about to play a few dirty tricks on us. These were the years of the laugh-packed 80's. A Hollywood actor was about to become president. America was on a roll—and after his return to L.A., Jerry was poised for take-off, even if the bare necessities of life were still hard to come by on the Sunset Strip. We burned up the phone lines after Jerry got a small part on

Benson, a sitcom spin-off from *Soap*. The *Benson* series starred actor Robert Guillaume as a butler who served a bumbling state governor too virtuous for his own good.

Jerry was cast as Frankie, a joke-telling messenger, and it seemed at first that this role might be exactly the sort of break he'd been waiting for. He made four thousand dollars per episode but, soon after shooting his fourth, he returned to New York with a horror story. We met in the City to catch up on the latest. Over pizza at Tom's, Jerry glumly lamented to me that he had been fired from *Benson* and that nobody had even bothered to tell him about it. He had apparently shown up like usual one day for a reading of the script, and an assistant director had called him aside to give him the bad news. Naturally, Jerry had been devastated. But we tried to put a positive spin on it, speculating that he had simply been too funny and upstaged the star of the show.

I told Jerry, "You were stealing Robert Guillaume's laughs. You can't let it get to you. You'll land something better next time."

Jerry vowed he would never do another role on a series unless he had total control. He wasn't going to put himself at the mercy of others again. This was a bitter experience, and I had no doubt he was serious.

Later, I confessed to Jerry that I had decided to give up acting for a while. At the time my mother died, I had been rehearsing an off-off-Broadway production of *When You Comin' Back, Red Ryder?* I was producing the show at the Wonderhorse Theatre in the East Village but, in my grief, I was forced to close before the curtain ever went up. After the wake, it seemed like my world had been turned upside down and shaken. Marie and I moved in together, first sharing an apartment in Queens, then pursuing plans to buy a house together. Now I had to consider the daunting possibility of settling down and getting married, even though I hadn't proposed. I told Jerry that for once in my life I wanted to have a steady income. I insisted, "It's time for me to get serious. I can always go back to acting."

Jerry could see it was breaking my heart, and he did his best to console me. At that moment I admired and envied him simply for being steadfast in chasing after his dreams. While he was still in town, Marie and I opened a deli in Queens, the first in a string of checkered Costanza enterprises; like George, I had my difficulties working for anyone, even myself. I named the deli "Mrs. C's" after my mother. Jerry's father, Kal, made bright Day-Glo signs for the specialty meats and cheeses that we offered. I hung his signs over the counter, touched by the fact that he had made them a gift. On the day of our grand opening, Jerry visited to wish me good luck, and to say good-bye before taking another shot at L.A.

When he came into the deli, I was behind the counter with my father and two uncles, Nat and Russ. Jerry brought along a potted plant to put in the front window. After he set it down, I honored him with the first-ever International Prosciutto Award, explaining that it was intended for comics on the rise. With as much pomp as I could muster, I handed him a little pyramid of Italian ham with ribbons streaming from it. He said mischievously, "I really can't accept this without thanking all those who made it possible."

The prosciutto set him off, and he made a grand tour of the store, aisle by aisle. At one point, he stepped around behind the counter and picked up some headcheese. Wrinkling his nose like he was utterly baffled, he asked, "What exactly is headcheese anyway? It's not cheese, and it's not a head. I mean, does this make any sense? Oh, here's a good one...tongue! What exactly is tongue? And people buy this stuff?"

With fits and starts, he slowly improvised his way through the store like he was taking inventory. He hit upon a box of Grape-Nuts cereal, and said, "And what about this?—it's not grapes, and it's not nuts—what is it?"

Aside, my father asked me, "Jerry doesn't know what head-cheese is?"

I said, "How many years have you known him, Pop? He's Jerry. He doesn't know headcheese."

He may not have bought anything that afternoon, but he gave my family something which we all knew came from the heart. And he had some new bits to take with him on the road.

When we said good-bye outside, I gave him a hug and kidded him about going west again. I said, "Just remember what my grandmother used to tell me—Every good-bye ain't gone...every shut-eye ain't sleepin'...and every how-d'ya-do ain't glad-to-meet-ya." I added, "She could say it in Italian."

Suddenly, he was Bud Abbott again, just shaking his head.

When he headed down the sidewalk, I yelled after him, "And don't forget...believe half of what you see, none of what you hear."

Turning back, he asked, "Who said that?"

"Uncle Sal," I told him.

* * *

A new ritual was established. Whenever Jerry came into town, either to perform or just to visit, he would phone me and "connect" as he called it. I would call our old friends and ask them to meet us for a night out or for one of Jerry's performances. The friends included Jesse, Joey Bacino, and another Italian-American friend of ours from Brooklyn, Anthony D'Alto, or "D," as we called him. While Jerry was gone, I stayed away from the club scene, except for some nights spent carousing or club-hopping with comedian Larry Miller, one of Jerry's favorite comics and a friend to us both (Larry would later appear in the title role of the *Seinfeld* episode "The Doorman").

The early turning point for Jerry came in 1981 when a talent scout saw his stand-up act and he received his first invitation to appear on Johnny Carson's *Tonight Show*. Over the phone, Jerry told me that he turned the offer down. He didn't think he was ready and was afraid of failing on the show. He'd seen this happen to one of his competitors on the circuit, a comic named David Cey who had disappeared after bombing the second time that he appeared on the *Tonight Show*, never to be heard from again.

Joking around, I said to Jerry, "Look, David Cey killed the first time he was on Carson. So he had the big fish in the boat, but he let it jump back in the water. Just don't do what he did. Hang on to your fish!"

Jerry knew it was the only kind of career advice he was ever going to get from me. Later in the year, he had a change of heart and made his debut on the *Tonight Show*. Marie and I sent a bouquet of balloons to the greenroom that day. The card read: "From The Golden Lion to Carson—Wow! Kill 'em, Jerry! Much love, Marie and Mike."

The date was May 7, 1981. Jerry had just turned twenty-seven on April 29th. Marie and I watched the show that night at our home in Queens. He walked on wearing blue slacks and a gray jacket, and he looked about as stylish and poised as I had ever seen him. The challenge for any comic appearing on the *Tonight Show* was to please Johnny Carson enough to win his acknowledgment after finishing the act. It might be a nod of approval. A wink. A handshake from the great man himself. However it finally came, this was the moment of supreme accomplishment every comedian was striving for, and Jerry was no exception.

He opened with a bit that questioned a driver checking under the hood of the car after a breakdown. Jerry asked, "What are you looking for? Whatever's wrong, you can't fix it. You stand there looking for something incredibly, obviously wrong—something so simple even you can handle it—a giant on/off switch!"

Then Jerry killed with a bit about Bob Hughes, listed as the world's heaviest man in the *Guinness Book of World Records*, weighing in at more than 1400 pounds. Jerry wondered what would happen if he lost a couple hundred pounds. "What would his friends say? You're a rail, baby, look at you!"

By the time that he speculated Bob Hughes would have to buy a whole new wardrobe, Jerry had Johnny Carson won over. At the end of the set, Johnny complimented him, saying, "Take a bow." These turned out to be the magic words that vaulted Jerry into the fast lane of comedy. His life would never be the same. Thanks to the time difference, I was able to phone in my congratulations before the show had even aired on the west coast.

But the ride to the top was not without its bumps.

The following year he came into New York to appear on David Letterman's late night show, which was then just getting underway on NBC. Jerry arranged for Jesse and me to go, and the two of us waited with Jerry in Letterman's "greenroom," while the show was being taped in the afternoon for broadcast that night. The greenroom was a waiting room with snacks and video monitors. Time was running out because another guest was milking his interview with Dave for all it was worth. Eventually, one of the producers came in and informed Jerry that he was "bumped"— there wasn't enough time for his spot. Then David Letterman himself came in, looking much more serious than I had ever seen him appear when he was on the show. Jesse and I watched expectantly as he said to Jerry, "I'm really sorry this happened. We'll reschedule you..."

Jesse cut in, teasing both Dave and Jerry, "Like my father says, you gotta get here early if you want to get on."

Everybody laughed, but it was the awkward kind of laughter that has tension in it. Jerry's managers quickly stepped in, more than happy to take over from here. Jerry was soon rescheduled, and Jesse and I returned weeks later to see him triumph. At the end of his routine that day, he was invited to have a seat next to Dave's desk and, as guest, he held his own through his first Letterman interview, nervous as he was.

At this point, Jerry and Dave were not equals—Dave was the one with power. This was evident, at least to me, as Jerry talked about his stand-up career to Dave, who had just graduated from the club circuit to host his own late-night spot.

After the show was taped, Jerry kept asking me, "How did I do? Honestly, what did you think?"

I told him the truth, saying, "You killed, Jerry. You killed them out there."

"Really?"

"Really!" I said.

He soaked in all the emotional reassurance he could, as if he didn't quite believe any of this was actually happening. These television appearances meant that Jerry could command a much higher price for club bookings. A short time after the Carson and Letterman shows, Jerry performed at Carnegie Hall as an opening act for a songstress named Laura Branigan, who was hot at the time with a hit single entitled, "Gloria."

Waiting with Jerry backstage at Carnegie that night before the show, I asked him, "So what are they paying you?"

He smiled and said, "You don't want to know."

"Come on," I said. "How much? I want to hear this."

"Why?" he asked, not really trying to hide anything, but making it into a game.

I patted his arm. "I'm your friend. Tell me what you're making. I want to be sure they're taking care of you."

Jerry said, "Twenty-five thousand."

I whistled and said, "That's a lot of headcheese."

Jerry stole the show that night even from the die-hard Laura Branigan fans. Afterwards, a large group of us went to Chinatown for dinner at the Mandarin Inn. As Jerry and I walked along Mott Street towards the restaurant, we passed a favorite Chinese joint from our college days—Wo Hop. This was where we used to go to guzzle down MSG at fabulous prices, where we could spend a dollar-eighty for a giant plate of beef with Chinese mushrooms and white rice. We had a lot of memories of the place and, as we passed it that night, I pointed out that the owner had just opened a second restaurant above.

I told Jerry, "So now there's two Wo Hops, one upstairs and one down. It's like they're starting a chain."

"Right," said Jerry. "I'll have the Wo Hopper!"

When we finally got a table and sat with our friends in the Mandarin Inn, a birthday party was in progress and an old record player was playing—hissing out a scratchy, Chinese rendition of "Happy Birthday." When the song finished, all of us clapped along with the Chinese family at the next table. But the needle skipped and the record started playing again. The birthday family was now in some confusion as to whether or not they should sing an encore. Jerry smiled and encouraged them to continue, saying, "It's okay, really! They're working their way down the block."

He knew how to punch the laugh buttons in every imaginable situation, though for some reason Jerry had some trouble with his delivery at weddings. As it turned out, Jesse was the first of us to go down and, in 1982, Jerry came home again to be a part of the bridal party, serving as an usher for Jesse. The festivities took place at a temple in Brooklyn and all of us sported yarmulkes for the occasion. As a minor celebrity for those assembled, Jerry was asked to perform some of his act at the reception. This was quite a spirited Jewish bash—a tough crowd, since a cocktail hour had started an hour before the ceremony. There was only a small, bare stage and Jerry was a few minutes into his show when some of the guests shushed him, motioning for Jerry to keep it down. But he carried on saying in a whisper, "I'm doing it as quietly as I can!"

Despite the cool reception he received for his performance, Jerry's visit gave him yet another gold mine of material. He had rented a standard tuxedo for the occasion and, having survived the rigors of the fitting and dealing with a bow tie, he would soon add a new joke to his routine on the outrageous, time-honored ritual of tuxedo rental: "There's a thrill—wearing a suit that's already been worn by eighty high school guys on the most exciting night their glands have ever known!"

Since I was Jesse's best man and made the customary toast to the bride and groom, Jerry polished off one more one-liner, taking me aside and asking, "If you're the *best* man, why is she marrying Jesse?"

The following year Jerry decided to test the marriage idea himself. He phoned me from the road to announce that he was engaged—she was a hotel manager, and he had known her for at least a month. I was at home in the kitchen when he called, and I cupped the phone with my hand to deliver the news to Marie. Then I asked him, "Are you sure this is the real thing and not just your pepino telling you what to do?"

He was petrified but still insisting that he was going to go through with it. He said, "It's like being on the roller coaster, and you can hear that chain clicking when you're on the way up to the top..."

"Great!" I enthused. "So you're ready to take the big dip. We can have a double wedding on a roller coaster!"

He laughed in a way that told me Jerry was in no danger of losing his bachelorhood. He was just going through the crisis of turning thirty. In his act he would quickly turn the whole affair into a "just-say-no" bit—the answer to breaking off engagements. I was the one who followed through by tying the knot when Marie and I married in 1984. The ceremony was performed in Manhattan at Marble Collegiate Church and the reception was held at Tavern On The Green. Jerry attended, as did the others in our faithful, fun-loving crew. He didn't perform, though he and Jesse were inspired at one point during the reception to stand together and chant the old Doublemint Gum jingle—using jars of grape jam as props. "It's two...two...two jams in one!"

As anybody watching us could tell, there were no depths to which we wouldn't stoop when cutting up. We enjoyed embarrassing ourselves and each other, and we were still playing the game of one-upmanship. We were still kids at heart.

In these small ways, I loved being a kind of secret sharer in Jerry's act and took great pride in watching his success, even with our lives moving in such totally different directions. I was still living in Queens; Jerry was everywhere, playing gigs three hundred nights a year. He had his place in L.A. as well as the old studio on 81st Street, where the machine usually answered when he was in town with Jerry's voice offering only the simplest of glib instructions: "You know what to do..." or "Go..."

During this take-off period, he came into town again to play a club called Bananas, which was part of a Holiday Inn in Fort Lee, New Jersey, just across the George Washington Bridge. Jerry called and told me to meet him in the greenroom, and I arrived in time to have dinner with him before he went on. His show that night was as polished as I had ever seen it. He did some old favorites like the socks, Tide, and computer dating, and some bits that I hadn't heard before. He commented on industrial-size popcorn in movie theaters: "I don't need that much roofing insulation!" He also pointed out the advantage of soap-on-a-rope: "It comes in handy. Sometimes I'm in the shower and I want to hang myself!"

The audience adored him. At the end of the night, a couple hundred people crowded outside the greenroom to ask Jerry for his autograph. The crush was unbearable, but he was graciously signing as many as he could. I stood by and tried to keep him from getting knocked down. There was a limousine waiting outside, and it seemed he was now living in the middle of madness like a rock star. When we finally made a getaway, I said, "It's Seinfeld Fever! You're like John, Paul, George and Ringo rolled into one!"

Jerry just laughed. He was low-key about it all. He said, "I'm only as good as my last show, Mike."

"Yeah, well, don't retire yet," I said.

He would perform on the Carson, Letterman, and Merv Griffin shows dozens of times, with each appearance adding a horde of new fans. On the circuit, Jerry and his friendly competitor, Jay Leno, had emerged as the hottest acts around. Seinfeld-mania had really started to build when Jerry's father, Kal, passed away during 1985. As the devoted son, Jerry felt the loss deeply. He called me from Florida where the funeral took place. I offered the only words of solace I could think of, remembering that before he first appeared on the *Tonight Show*, Kal had placed a huge sign on his truck and then drove all over Long Island announcing the big event. I reminded Jerry that he had made his father proud.

One night a few months later, after Marie and I had gone to sleep, the phone rang in our bedroom. I bobbled the receiver and then heard a familiar voice saying, "Mikey, it's Jerry. Are you there?"

"Hey, buddy," I said, still barely conscious. "Where are you calling from?"

He said he was playing someplace like Milwaukee or Cincinnati. "I'm back in the hotel. I just finished a set."

"Rough night?" I asked.

"No, not really. It's just the road, Mike. I wanted to hear a friendly voice. It gets a little lonely, you know?"

"Sure," I said.

"The show's over, and I don't feel like sleeping with anyone. I don't want to have to continue my performance. Sometimes I don't feel like being *on*, you know. I'm on all the time. It's great to be able to talk without the bull..." He asked how Marie was doing, knowing that she was expecting our first child, and both Jerry and I expressed astonishment that I was going to be a father. Serious discussions were rare with us and this one left a deep impression on me.

We talked for another ten minutes or so about things like the price of success, and loneliness. I didn't really know what he was going through, but the last thing I said was, "I'm glad you called, Jer. You know I'm here for you."

I saw Jerry again later in the year when he came to New York to play Caroline's Comedy Club on my thirtieth birthday, September 6. I was riding high at that time—my daughter, Mariel, had just been born, and my wife and I had sold the deli. We'd recently bought our first new home and established a modestly successful concession in Manhattan—Quiche A La Carte—a fleet of lunch carts serving quiche and Perrier. Wearing bright chef hats and pushing our carts under French umbrellas, we operated throughout the City for about a year until Mayor Koch ran most of the cart vendors off the streets. We switched over to lunch boxes featuring a popular item known as the "Quiche Cookie" which we successfully marketed around the country for another couple of years.

Marie and I were up to our ears with quiche when my birthday arrived. In the afternoon Jerry lugged a bonsai tree and clay pot to Queens as a house-warming gift for us. This was the first time he'd met my daughter so it was quite a celebration for all of us. Then Jerry brought Marie and me into the city for his show at Caroline's. I'll never forget his opening that night. After he was introduced onstage and the applause died down, Jerry said, "Ladies and gentleman, tonight is a special occasion—it's the thirtieth birthday of my best friend, Mike Costanza." Pointing to the table where my wife and I were sitting, Jerry said, "Please give Mike a hand..."

The entire audience sang "Happy Birthday" to me and, at that moment, I really did know what it meant to be touched beyond words. All I could do was hug him when he came offstage. Marie jokingly accused me of being too emotional. But that was just the Italian in me, I suppose.

Some months later Jerry went into the hospital for some minor knee surgery, and I sent an actor in a gorilla suit to his room to cheer him up—a gorilla-gram. He called after this little prank and was chuckling when I picked up the phone. He said, "It had to be you, Costanza!"

* * *

The following year I had to fly to L.A. for some meetings with supermarket executives about my quiche cookies. I paid a surprise visit to Jerry's West Hollywood apartment—an unannounced "stop-in." This was my first visit and I was staying a few blocks away with my actor brother, Joe. After one of my meetings, I walked to Jerry's place. No one walks in L.A., but I insisted, catching sight of the Hollywood sign on my way. There was the smell of jacaranda bushes as I came around the corner and walked up to the front door of his building. Jerry's face registered a seismic shock as soon as he opened his door—4.0 or 5.0 on the surprise scale.

When I saw how bare his apartment was, I told him, "Well, you don't have to worry about any flying objects in a quake. But when are you going to move in?"

He did have some clothes in the closet and a giant-screen TV. I asked about a little electronic gizmo that he had set up near his writing desk. "An oxidizer," Jerry said. Seeing my blank face, he waved an arm at the room and explained, "So it always smells like it just rained."

We had some good laughs that afternoon and then I had to fly home. I was pleased that I'd finally satisfied my curiosity about his L.A. living situation. After I thought about it, I realized that Jerry's bachelor pads, wherever he was living, always looked like hotel rooms. He was homeless.

In 1986 he came in for my birthday again, and this time it was a surprise party that Marie arranged, spending an extravagant sum to rent a yacht for four hours so that we could take a dozen friends out on the Hudson River. Champagne. Surf and turf. A deejay. A ride in the sunset. At one point, with the Statue of Liberty in view, Jerry and I sat in the cabin and steered the boat. I predicted, "One day you'll have one of these—you can park it at the 79th Street Boat Basin."

He said, "I don't know, Mike. That's a lot of coupons."

Jerry was already a millionaire. But this was not a guy that success could ever spoil. I was certain of that. Our relationship was the same as always. It was like a conversation that continued where it left off each time we saw each other.

A few months later we met for lunch with Jesse and our buddy Larry Miller at the Museum Cafe, a restaurant behind the Museum of Natural History and just around the corner from Jerry's 81st Street studio. I remember this meeting because there was so much I wasn't able to say. Marie and I were having to face some hard times with our quiche business going down the tubes because of some changes in Reagan's tax laws. We had lost our house and our cars and we had just learned that our daughter, Mariel, was autistic. Our roller coaster was in the dip and I wasn't saying much.

Ironically, the conversation turned to money and Jerry was telling us about the ludicrous fees he received when he was hired away from the clubs to play at conventions for companies like IBM. He had me laughing along in spite of myself. He said, "It's just crazy money—they don't know what they're supposed to pay the comedian. Forty or fifty grand for an hour."

I kidded him, saying to Jesse and Larry, "Sounds like Jerry money."

Tongue in cheek, Larry voiced his opinion that these killer fees were well-earned as he recalled playing a police convention and having to go onstage just after the audience had listened to the tragic testimonial of a crime victim.

We all agreed that it was a world gone crazy. After leaving the restaurant, Jesse and I walked through Central Park with Larry and Jerry, who were meeting Jay Leno on the East Side. Jay was much admired by Jerry and Larry for both his shrewd career moves and comic style, and all three had become friends. For his own career guidance, Jerry was now placing great faith in his personal manager, George Shapiro, who also represented Carl Reiner and Andy Kaufman. Jerry would later tell me that it was George Shapiro who lent a first name to Costanza, but at this time he was setting up Jerry's first HBO special, *Jerry Seinfeld: Stand-Up Confidential*, a spoof on how comedians get their material.

Heading east through the park, Jerry and I walked in front and he zeroed in on my mood, pinning me down on how things were going. I didn't want to burden him with anything so distant from his world. I only admitted that my quiche business had gone into a tailspin for me. Larry jumped into the middle, saying, "Mike, we know you're already planning your next move. You're the kind who always rolls the dice with big *cajones*."

Jerry took my arm and said, "Don't let it get to you, Mikey. You've got more going for you than quiche!"

We parted with a hug, and Jerry asked, "You're okay?"

"Yeah, sure," I told him. "I'll bounce back. You know me."

As Jesse and I walked back to the West Side through the park, I spilled the rest of the story to him. By now Jesse had moved up the career ladder and was working for one of the networks. But he was still more in my league as far as dealing with the nitty-gritty of life's rolling dice, especially when they came up craps. I told Jesse my plan was to put together a few pennies and go into another business. I said, sadly, "I need the *scarole*. You know what it's like being married. I want to go back to acting, but it's out of the question now."

Happily, I did bounce back with all of the survival instincts of George Costanza. I soon got into high-volume gourmet salads, my own Vandelay Industries. Of course, this was before either George or I went into the real estate business.

* * *

One day in the summer of 1988 Jerry phoned me from his newly purchased apartment in Manhattan and left a message on my machine. I had been out playing racquetball with Jesse, and I returned the call when I came in. As soon as Jerry answered the phone, I said, "Hey, Tutti Finute, how's it going?"

He said, "Mike, I'm on the way out..."

"Yeah, sure," I broke in. "I knew this comedy thing wouldn't last."

He snickered and invited me to stop by the next day now that he had finished renovating his new place. We agreed on lunch, and I said I would bring Jesse and Joey Bacino. "What's the address?" I asked.

"230 Central Park South."

"Pretty fancy," I said. "I hope they let us in. How much did this place set you back?"

Jerry said, "Three million and another four hundred big ones to renovate."

"That's a lot of jokes!" I told him. "Maybe we should throw you a benefit."

Jerry laughed and said, "You're not kidding. I'm tapped out. See ya tomorrow."

That same afternoon Marie and I went to nearby Bayside to hunt for an apartment-warming gift for Jerry. In the window of a little shop, I spotted a yellow and white Lucite clock that I liked. This was a 15-minute clock—a novelty based on Andy Warhol's notion of 15 minutes of fame. Marie and I discussed the possibility of Jerry misinterpreting the gift. We didn't want him to think that we were suggesting his minutes of success might be numbered, so we made sure to explain in our card that the clock was intended to mark his *next* 15 minutes of stardom. Then we packed the clock in one of the little shopping bags designed for those of us who are gift-wrapping impaired.

The next day I drove into the City, picking up Jesse and Joey on the way. We caught a lucky parking spot on the Upper

West Side and parked near Central Park West. Jerry lived in a handsome, well-kept building with a large awning in front—The Wendover. The three of us went into the lobby and gave our names to a uniformed concierge who called upstairs saying, "Mr. Seinfeld, a Mike, Jesse, and Joey are here to see you...Thank you, sir."

He sent us to the elevator, directing us to the fourteenth floor. Once the door closed, the three of us only had to look at each other before we burst out laughing like we were suddenly back in school. What sort of nest had our old pal landed in? When we rang the bell of 14-C, we heard a normal-sounding buzzer. Joey said, "That's the bell you get for three million?"

Jesse asked, "What were you expecting, some heavenly angels singing *Ave Maria*?"

We were cackling when Jerry opened the door. He hugged each of us as we made our way inside. He said, with a clipped English accent, "Welcome to my humble abode." I was the last inside, and he asked me, "What's so funny?"

"We just thought for three mill they'd give you a better bell. Are you gonna give us the tour?"

"Sure..." He started to show us around, but we soon split up, roaming from room to room. Although Jerry had indeed moved in, the place reflected his usual style. There were enormous bookshelves, empty except for a pile of shaving gear.

I said, "Jerry the minimalist has been at it again."

"You know me," he said. "No distractions, Mikey."

The only distractions in the living room were wrap-around windows overlooking Central Park. The floors were hardwood, and they glistened under his white Nikes. When the two of us walked into the kitchen, I exclaimed, "Wow! Sub-zero fridge. Gaggenau stove."

Jerry said, "Yeah, give me your professional opinion."

"Not bad, my friend. Top of the line. Marie would kill for this setup." I opened the refrigerator as Jesse and Joey came into the kitchen. I said, "Hey, look, guys. It's freakin' empty!" I turned to Jerry and said, "This is like having a Porsche with no gas."

Laughing happily, he said, "I'm taking you guys out to lunch anyway."

Jesse opened a side cabinet inside the fridge and said, "At least he's got beer." Passing a bottle of beer, he asked Jerry, "So how do you like living at the Wendover?"

Jerry smirked and said, "With what I paid for it, it's more like the Bendover."

His line elicited guffaws all around, and whatever tension there had been when we first arrived now vanished. It was as if Jerry had clicked into some old familiar rhythm. We walked back into the living room, and I handed him my gift in a shopping bag, saying, "Here's a little something from me and Marie."

He accepted graciously. Then he pulled the tissue paper out and said, "Mike, I'm sorry...you know I only use Scott."

We prodded him, and he pulled out the clock. He looked at it, and then he looked at me. Then he said, "Are you trying to tell me my time is up?"

I told him, "Marie knew you'd say that. I meant...there's a card..."

He said, "I know what you meant. Thanks, Mikey." He placed the clock on the mantle above the fireplace. Coming around again, he asked, "How 'bout some music?"

We all encouraged him, and he put some cool jazz on the sound system. I asked, "Crusaders?"

"Spyro Gyra," Jerry said.

I said, "Getting very sophisticated, aren't we?"

Joey said, "I guess *In-A-Gadda-Da-Vida* just doesn't make it here."

Jerry picked up a set of binoculars from a small table and handed them to Jesse, saying, "Check these out. The latest toy. They go for over a grand."

Jesse walked to one of the shimmering windows and raised the binoculars, saying, "For that much money I want to be able to see under their clothes."

Another round of laughs.

Jerry suggested that we sneak up to the roof of the building

94

for the view. We brought along our beers and soon found ourselves heading out onto the landing on the top floor. There was a wall of impatiens and beyond that a bird's-eye view of Central Park. The sun was pouring down on us like a shower of jewels. Jesse said, "It's like being in a helicopter up here."

I told Jerry, "It's better than looking out at tar beach," referring to the view of the rooftop that he'd had at his 81st Street studio.

We all toasted him with our beers, and sensing a celebration, Jerry casually told us that NBC had approached him with an offer to star in his own comedy series. "I should have more control than in the past," he said, meaning *Benson*. He went on to explain that the new offer had come from Brandon Tartikoff, the head of the network. Naturally, we pressed Jerry to fill in the details about the show.

"Wow, that's great!" I said. "What's it about?"

"Well," he said, "I'll do some stand-up at the beginning of each episode—material based on that night's show."

"Yeah, sounds good," I said. "But what's it about?"

"It's about these guys who live in a building in Manhattan. They do things that are funny, you know, whatever comes up."

"Like what?"

"Whatever...it's hard to explain. The little things that we deal with all the time."

I said, "So these guys are just hanging out?"

"Yeah," said Jerry, "They hang out. One of them is a comic. So I do stand-up. I'm basically playing myself and the other guys are my friends."

"But what do they do?" I asked, really trying to understand. "Do they do anything special?"

"Nothing special," he insisted.

"They must do something," I said.

"No, it's just about their everyday lives in New York. They don't really do anything."

"So they're doing nothing," I said. "You're writing a show about some guys who don't know who they are or what they're doing? You're writing a show about nothing special? That means nothing?"

"Right," said Jerry, getting into this banter and grinning from ear to ear, always ready to play along.

Jesse said, "This sounds like 'Who's on first'," referring to the classic Abbott and Costello routine.

Jerry had us going now, and he knew it. We were like his own personal test audience.

"Even a show about nothing has to be about something," I told him. "You must have characters and plots." I looked at Jesse and Joey to see if they thought that Jerry was as crazy on this one as I did. "Guys, we're gonna watch a show about nothing?" Gesturing to Jerry with my beer bottle, I asked, "Is this a done deal?"

"Yeah," he said. "We get a pilot and four-shot test. If the network buys it, then we'll get a year. You remember Larry David from The Improv?"

"Sure," I said. "That comic who used to get pissed at the audience when they didn't get his jokes. Very angry guy all the time."

Jerry snickered and said, "Yeah, he's writing it with me. Larry's very funny. Trust me. It's gonna be great."

I eyed him suspiciously and said, "Network prime time. Your life's gonna change forever...you know that, don't you?"

"What do you mean?" he asked.

I said, "You'll have three times as many people watching as you get on Carson or Letterman. You won't be able to go outdoors. You'll be mobbed all the time."

He said, "People are usually pretty nice. They don't bother me much. They usually just nod or smile when they pass me on the street."

"Yeah, right," I said, thinking of some of the times I had seen him accosted.

Jerry was right that day; when all of us went to lunch and strolled on Columbus Avenue, nobody intruded on his privacy. We chatted about the usual nothing and checked out the action on the street. After we'd walked Jerry back to his building, we all said our good-byes and wished him good luck. The last thing I said was, "Don't forget to let us know when the show is gonna be on. We'll be watching, pal."

Chapter Five

Showdown

Once Jerry started working full-time on the show, it seemed more and more that we were leading parallel lives, with him in L.A. most of the time and me in New York. We kept up with each other at a distance, linked in surreal fashion by the *Seinfeld* series itself—by those images on the TV screen depicting the world he had almost succeeded in leaving behind, not that he had ever wanted to. The times Jerry was able to come into New York usually fell between April and July, from the end of one *Seinfeld* production season to the start of the next. It was like he had to return at least once a year, if only for a reality check.

As many devoted *Seinfeld* fans know, the pilot episode was entitled "The Seinfeld Chronicles"—which was also the original name of the series. The show first aired July 5th, 1989 and all of my family and all the old gang watched in a state of jubilation. After all, Jerry was one of our own, like a favorite son, our very own joke-spinning Superboy who refused to grow up. We rooted for him like his hometown rooted for him, because Jerry's star had touched our more conventional lives.

I told my father and the whole Costanza tribe to watch the pilot and expect a surprise. Thanks to the sentimental messages that Jerry left beforehand on my answering machine, I knew he had named his best friend on the show after me. I couldn't have been more thrilled by his gesture. The idea that my family name would be immortalized on prime time TV was a tremendous kick for all of us, even for some of my young cousins, who called from Brooklyn after the show to say they didn't think Jerry was funny, and couldn't figure out what the show was about.

After offering Jerry a more favorable review, my father said to me prophetically, "Maybe he'll put you and your brother on the show." Then he added, as the Costanza patriarch, "He should have just hired you...to be you!"

"No, Pop," I told him. "That guy Jason Alexander is great. They've got a terrific actor playing me."

My father always had the last word. "They shoulda hired the real Costanza."

I was stunned to see Jerry just playing himself and not some sitcom character. There was my old buddy on the little screen, the same guy I had known all these years. The sensation could not have been more strange—it really was Jerry Through the Looking Glass, and I was somewhere between amazed and thunderstruck.

One situation in the pilot episode was very familiar to me, with George and Jerry as sidekicks driving to the airport to pick up Jerry's most recent romantic fantasy, a woman who unfortunately turned out to be engaged. The bantering rapport between these two pals had me identifying with George in a big way, and I laughed at the parts of myself that I saw in him. I couldn't resist needling Jerry, saying, "How many times in our lives have we driven around like that?" We chatted on the phone after each of the early episodes, with NBC unveiling the four test shows in the spring of 1990.

The biggest change after the pilot was the addition of the female character, Elaine. NBC executives had insisted on a woman to balance the three-man act, and Jerry had come up with the idea of Elaine as the ex-girlfriend who was now the buddy for Jerry, George, and Kramer.

As far as the network was concerned, the fate of *Seinfeld* was still in doubt when the third episode, "The Robbery," aired on June 7th. The plot involved a burglary at Jerry's apartment when he was out of town, calling to my mind the actual burglaries that occurred at Jerry's 81st Street studio. In this same episode, George showed Jerry a luxurious new apartment for rent, then turned on his pal when he decided he wanted to take the place himself. This wasn't something I would have done, and yet it was funny, as Jerry pointed out, with the two of them finally flipping a coin for it—only to end up losing the place after being overheard by a waitress. This sort of cutthroat thing was familiar to many of us New Yorkers.

Had I been more perceptive or clairvoyant, I might have been able to envision from this one episode how George would develop as a character, with his scheming, dark side. But I wasn't yet aware of the contribution Jerry's co-writer, Larry David, was making to the Costanza portrayal.

The *Seinfeld* test episodes had not done well in the ratings but the show did have some influential supporters. With the help of director Rob Reiner at Castle Rock Entertainment (the producers of *Seinfeld*) and Rick Ludwin, one of the heads at NBC, the network gave the show a green light. The first full season was to run in 1992. From that point on, Jerry's fate was sealed, and in a way, so was mine.

My personal roller coaster had been jolted by another series of dips. My father passed away unexpectedly, and Jerry and I were reunited in Queens for the funeral. I was grateful he had come but especially sorry to have to see him under the circumstances. I had recently opened a deli in the City on 14th Street only to be driven out of business when construction on the block shut down traffic in the area—killing the Costanza deli. This one had been named for my father, Joe—"J.C.'s."

Still, I wasn't undone as George might have been, and I suppose I derived some spiritual strength from it all. Some months after pulling out of my dips and recovering from the losses, I told Jerry that Marie and I were planning a move to Long Island. Costanza in the kingdom of malls? He was greatly amused and accused me over the phone, with his usual sardonic wit, "You're joining the witness protection program?"

But there were reasons for my move that I soon explained to him. On the day that I'd closed the deli, my former acting teacher, Anthony Mannino, came in by chance for a slice of pizza.

Tony had always been an inspiration of mine, and he had convinced me to return to my acting career. To give myself enough flexibility to attend auditions and rehearsals, I had now decided to relocate to the suburbs and take a job selling real estate. I told Jerry, "Well, if I can't pitch for the Yankees, at least I can make my own hours...so I have time to act again."

Jerry said, "So you're an actor selling real estate."

"Yeah," I said. Then I allowed my pride to say, kiddingly, "Watch out, Seinfeld. I'm just one audition away from being up there with you."

When I later saw George quit his real estate job over being refused the use of his boss's private bathroom, I knew that Jerry was making a private joke, combining my experience in real estate with one of my quirky bathroom idiosyncrasies. Jerry knew all about my eccentric preference for using "home base" facilities. During our college days, he had teased me about my reluctance to work too far from home, where the comforts of space and bathroom luxury had been lovingly provided by Italian craftsmen. That bathroom in the basement was a 15x30-foot palace, and the first time Jerry saw the oversized, tiled room, he dubbed it "the Costanza mausoleum," pointing out: "You have enough room in here for urinals!"

George's exit from his real estate job occurred during "The Revenge" episode, which aired April 18, 1991. My life came up on this same show in another way when Kramer put quick-drying cement into a washing machine because he and Jerry suspected the laundry-man of taking some money Jerry left in a pocket of his dirty laundry. This incident was identical to one of my high school pranks that the real Jerry had known about for years. So it became obvious to me early on that he was reaching into my past for some of the show ideas, just as he had created some of his stand-up bits when our conversations or the events in our lives set him off.

It was as if he was performing his magic under my nose and once again, in these small ways, I was secretly flattered to be a part of the act.

I was also happy to have returned to performing again

myself. I was hired as an extra on *The Godfather, Part III*, and spent three days in Little Italy being entertained as I waited for my scene and watched the charismatic John Gotti, who stayed on the fringe of the action like he was trying to insinuate himself with the movie crowd. I also had the chance to see Pacino and Coppola at work. It was great fun, and then I was cast in the lead role for an off-off-Broadway production of *Savage Wilds* at the Nuyorican Poet's Cafe. Not unexpectedly, Jerry had to decline my invitation to attend. He was in L.A. and explained to me on the phone, "Mike, I'm as busy as a one-armed paper-hanger. The show's taking over my life!"

I asked him, "So how does it feel to finally be a made man?"

He just laughed.

As it happened in the winter of 1991, Jerry did invite me to play a small part on the show. The episode he had in mind for me was called "The Subway," and Jerry wanted me to act the role of a character that Kramer overheard in the subway giving a tip on a racehorse. Unfortunately, I wasn't able to get away from my job in time to make the trip to L.A.

"Costanzarized!" I said to myself, at least a thousand times after having to turn Jerry down.

That show aired a couple months later, on January 8, 1992, and that was when funny things started happening. Marie and I watched the episode in our Long Island living room, and it was George who caught our attention soon after the opening scenes. By this time, Marie and our friends and families were basically looking at me as George in my real life. It was assumed we were one and the same simply because everyone knew about Jerry and me. So when George was conned by an enticing seductress in the subway and ended up being lured to a hotel room, then tied to a bed and robbed, I had some explaining to do.

Marie said, "Just tell me it didn't happen, Mike."

I managed to allay my wife's concerns that night, but a few of our friends phoned to heckle me. One of them said, "Since when are you chasing after women like that, Costanza?"

One of my uncles asked me seriously, "Did they ever catch her? Did you get your wallet and suit back, Mike?"

I figured this show had to have been some sort of aberration. I knew that Jerry hadn't used me as a source for this misadventure, and I was sure that he had never fallen victim in quite that way. But it didn't really dawn on me how the tale had been invented. Little did any of us know that I now had a dark twin—and so did George. It was like this person I identified with had a split personality. There was a new side of George that wasn't me.

I was struck by troubling thoughts: Is that how people see me? Can I really be such a loser? I may have run a few scams in my time, but I never prided myself on being a liar, let alone the "Lord of Idiots." George was only a minor irritation when life was going well for me and my family. But during the hard times, or on particularly bad days, George was like a plague on the Costanza house, chipping away at my self-esteem.

I didn't say anything to Jerry about it. How could I? It certainly wasn't anything he intended. As George's greed and selfishness became more apparent on successive episodes in 1992, I was torn. I was now getting more disturbing comments from friends and relatives, and even from some of my real estate associates. Each week it was something new. Pieces of me were obviously George, undeniably George—causing total confusion.

And the show was funny. By this time, there was a faithful cult following. Just as Marie and I were becoming concerned about the whole crazy case of mistaken identity, Jerry called to offer me the part on "The Parking Space." While I was out in L.A. filming the episode, I really did fall in love with the entire cast. Marie was expecting our second daughter at the time, and both Jason Alexander and Julia Louis-Dreyfus were also expectant parents when I visited. Jerry was his charming self, and so, after one attempt to broach the subject of George, I'd given up on the idea. What was the point?

Though I didn't make much money on the role after paying for the trip, at least I'd been working as an actor. I owed Jerry for that. One of the other people I met in the studio was Larry David, who greeted me on my first day just like the other actors had, "Oh, right, you're the real Costanza." Larry seemed like a nice enough guy, so it was hard to believe he was the one twisting George into a caricature of me.

Who was I to complain? I figured the show had become a hit and George was popular. Many in the audience loved him even with all his faults and peccadilloes. So, after I returned to New York, I decided to simply count myself lucky. Why had I wanted so much to talk to Jerry about George anyway? My wife had encouraged me because of her worries. But what on earth could Jerry have done, even if he had known what we were going through with George?

"It's not that bad," I told Marie, almost believing myself. "Some weeks he's just me."

"Yeah," said my wife, "and some weeks he's not!"

In this ludicrous situation, one moment I would find myself saying, "I am George," and the next moment, protesting, "I am not George!" Some readers may know Leonard Nimoy's books—*I Am Not Spock* and *I Am Spock*. It was like that for me, except I chose to remain behind the scenes. When I later saw Kenny Kramer come out of the woodwork as the "real Kramer," I wasn't tempted to follow his footsteps into the tabloids. Kenny Kramer was a former comic who had once lived across the hall from Larry David. Apparently, Kramer was paid by the producers to sign a release for the use of his name. I knew things were out of hand when I saw him running his campaign for mayor of New York City a few years later. What was the world coming to?

Meanwhile, Carol Leifer was identified by the media as the "real Elaine." I knew of a mystery woman who appeared to be another important real-life inspiration for Elaine, an L.A. model named Susan McNabb who dated Jerry on and off for a number of years after he'd ended his engagement back in 1984. Susan offered Jerry a number of personal stories and, before the series first aired, the Elaine character was named Susan. Jerry chose not to mention her or me in public. As he kept his social life in New York separate from his social life in L.A., I never met Susan. I felt a special bond with her, if only because she worked as a successful hand model; I'd put in a stint as a hand model for the Sports Channel during 1992. This may explain how a year later George found his way into this unusual field. Obviously, fate and sitcoms work in mysterious ways.

As time went on and the show became the hit of hits, Larry David allowed himself to be identified as George, and Jerry went along with the ruse. I joked about it with Marie one night after seeing Jerry interviewed. I said, "How many bald best friends who went to Queens College and hung out with him on the circuit do you think Jerry had?" Doing my best to imitate Jason Alexander's frantic histrionics, I told Marie, "It's getting to be like the Warren Commission—there's a *Seinfeld* cover-up!"

By this time, my wife was thinking that George was a dirty trick Jerry had played on me. I tried to keep a sense of humor about it; and to be fair, so did Marie.

On May 15, 1992, shortly after I returned from L.A. and "The Parking Space" aired, Jerry played at Carnegie Hall and arranged backstage passes for some of his friends, including me and Jesse, Larry Miller, Joey Pacino, Tony D'Alto, and Chris Misiano. Once the entire group of us assembled outside the hall, we fought through the crowd to get backstage, and then rode up in a service elevator with Barbara Walters, who was preparing to interview our pal. Barbara got off the elevator with us and we walked into a backstage area where a noisy party was already underway. Jerry spotted us from across the room and the crowd parted as he hurried over to greet us, all eyes following him.

He was like a fighter who had just been crowned champion, and he came straight at me, crying, "Mikey, what is that on your head!"

It was the first time he had seen my rug. I gave him a look, and said, "What? You don't like it?"

"No, no, it's great," said Jerry, trying not to bust a gut as he played his usual straight man on this one. With a huge grin, he said, impishly, "You can't tell. Really! I'd never have guessed. Very natural."

He gave me a bear hug. Then he stepped back and stared at the top of my head until he couldn't help laughing. He said, "How long have you had that thing?"

I said, "I bought it with the money I made on the show."

More laughter and another embrace.

With Barbara Walters waiting in the wings, he hugged each of us guys very emotionally. Joey Pacino told Jerry, "You've finally made it!"—and the rest of us chimed in loudly.

When the time came, I wished Jerry a killer night out there and left with the others to find our seats in the house.

Michael Richards opened the show for Jerry, masquerading as a spastic stage hand, carrying the mike, a stool, and glass of water onto the stage. He tangled himself in the mike cord, then took an outrageous fall over the stool. Michael's antics had the sold-out crowd going wild even before Jerry made his entrance. Then it was Seinfeld-mania as I had never seen it before. The audience was in hysterics from the first moment the lights dimmed and Jerry walked onto the stage until he took his bow.

He received a frenzied standing ovation. In little more than an hour, he managed to perform most of his tried and true routines. It was like listening to Seinfeld's Greatest Hits, joke after joke, from socks to dry cleaning to father-controlled thermostats, until it was too painful to laugh anymore.

Jerry was great, but at this point, he was no longer just a comic—he had become a phenomenon. He probably could have read from a phone book and gotten laughs, especially in New York City, the sacred home-turf of his biggest fans.

As the crowd started leaving, Jesse asked me, "How many times do you think we've laughed at the same jokes?"

I said, "He gets better and better. It's like he's an actor, and he's doing a play with a twenty-year run. But there's always something new with Jerry."

After the show, all of us went out to dinner at one of the trendy restaurants near Jerry's old apartment. We were ecstatic and celebrated until the very wee hours. It was like old times again with all the clowning and bantering.

In these situations, I felt like nothing had changed between us, and yet we were changing. I could tell by the way we checked out each other's faces for wrinkles, then ribbed each other about those waistlines and hairlines—the old gang was getting older, although Jerry sometimes seemed ageless and the camera loved him.

The night had been unforgettable for all of us. My wife and I had to laugh again months later when we watched a new episode of *Seinfeld* in which Jerry saw George wearing his toupé for the first time. The show was hilarious—the real Jerry obviously couldn't resist making the hairpiece into another bit for George. After the show, Marie and I didn't say a word to each other. We checked on the kids and then went through our usual nightly routine before going to bed. But as my head hit the pillow, Marie asked me, with only a hint of her good-hearted sarcasm, "Why didn't he just film it at Carnegie Hall when he was there with you?"

* * *

In the fall of 1992, Marie and I joined a church near our home in Holtsville. I became acquainted with the pastor and told him about my friendship with Jerry. I said that I had been on the show that year, and suggested to him that he might want to watch the next episode. He said he didn't watch much TV these days. Too much violence and bad taste. I encouraged him, saying, "It's a different kind of show. Clean jokes. Most people think it's very funny. You might enjoy it."

The pastor promised to give it a try. At the time, *Seinfeld* was on Wednesday nights, and Marie and I tuned in again that week as usual. The episode was called "The Contest." You can imagine our shock as we sat trying to envision our new pastor's reaction when we saw George explaining how he'd been caught by his mother in the bathroom with a copy of *Glamour*, just doing what came naturally to him. In the excitement, Mrs. Costanza fell and had to be taken to the hospital. George's account of this little incident eventually led to a contest between Jerry, George,

Kramer, and Elaine to see which of them could hold out the longest without giving in to the irresistible urge.

As it turned out, George and Jerry tied, succumbing at the same moment, after Kramer and Elaine had dropped out of the race. When the show was over, my wife said to me, "You'll never learn, will you? Why do you have to keep telling people?"

I never discussed the episode with our pastor, but the next Sunday as I sat in church listening to his sermon, I was sure the hand of God was going to reach down from heaven to give me a wedgie I'd never forget.

"The Contest" won an Emmy Award for Larry David in 1993 for Outstanding Writing in a Comedy Series.

* * *

Jerry was busier and wealthier. He had published a book of humor, *SeinLanguage*, and he'd also become a pitchman for American Express. He now had his collections of Porsches and Nike sneakers. After Carnegie Hall, he and one of his comic buddies, Mario Joyner, made a trip to Europe, visiting among other attractions, a Porsche factory in Germany. Jerry had little time to send postcards from the glamorous edge, but this was not someone success had spoiled. Stolen or abducted, maybe, but not spoiled.

Jerry's reputation for finicky neatness and cleanliness was already becoming a part of the legend. I teased him at one point on the phone, asking him lightheartedly, "What are you trying to be, the next Howard Hughes? Try being a little sloppy sometime."

The odd couple to the end.

He was single-minded on his path. Or almost. His manager, George Shapiro, had become a father figure, the able mastermind behind each of Jerry's career moves. There were a lot of other very funny comedians, as Jerry admitted, but few had their own shows skyrocketing in the ratings. George Shapiro helped build *Seinfeld* into a small empire.

Jerry was putting in sixteen-hour days. There was no longer a steady woman in his life, but sometimes he found himself splashed in the tabloids for having been caught on one of his brief flings. After I read he was seeing sex kitten Tawny Kitain, I asked about the story in passing. Jerry told me, not giving away anything I hadn't already imagined, "Well, we had a dabble."

"So," I pressed him, "how'd it go?"

He laughed and said, "I felt like I was in the presence of greatness, Mikey..."

We left it at that.

Jerry was something of a serial heartbreaker, but he always tried to be a friend to those he disappointed. He was honest and, over the years, had turned his reluctance to commit to a woman into a fabulous bit, embellishing his just-say-no routine with a telling observation about how to get off the roller coaster before getting trapped into a wedding date: "I can't be there...I've got my Fear of Commitment classes that week, and my I Don't Want to Grow Up training seminar..."

There were other tabloid controversies, one with Roseanne Barr involving *Seinfeld*, Scientology, and a parking space. The squabble became an ongoing joke. At the time, Roseanne and her husband, Tom Arnold, were doing ABC's hit, *Roseanne*. While not a Thursday night competitor, she attacked *Seinfeld*, saying, "They think they're doing Samuel Beckett instead of a sitcom." I think Jerry took this as an unintended compliment, but she also tried to tar and feather him as a Scientology cultist and branded Julia Louis-Dreyfus a "bitch" on David Letterman's show one night.

It all finally came down to a parking spot. Julia had stolen Tom Arnold's officially designated parking place at the studio lot one day. Hell hath no fury like a scorned victim of parking space theft! I asked Jerry about Roseanne, and he chuckled, saying only, "Blown out of proportion." I knew he wasn't trying to cut her down. Jerry rarely harbored bitterness or ill will toward anyone.

In the spring of 1993, I phoned Jerry's place one night and was surprised to hear the voice of radio shock-jock Howard Stern on Jerry's answering machine asking me to leave a message. A few days later I met Jerry for one of our impromptu catch-up lunches at the Museum Cafe. I was curious and asked, "So what's this you've got going with Howard Stern?"

Jerry replied a bit defensively, "What? Howard's a good guy. He can be very funny. You know, his ratings are high. So if I do his show, it helps my show."

I knew that Howard Stern was famous for ambushing his guests, even his friends. I cautioned Jerry about him, which was unusual for me, saying as gently as I could, "I hope he doesn't come back to bite you on the ass. You know what my grandmother used to say: Pigs grow fat, and hogs get slaughtered."

Shortly thereafter, Jerry and I talked on the phone and made a date to play some ball in Central Park. The weather looked good and I waited to hear back from him that afternoon before taking off for the City. But I didn't get a call until much later that night. It was a case of mixed signals and he was phoning to apologize. "Sorry I missed you, Mikey. But I went to the park, and I met this really incredible girl. She was with some of her girlfriends. You know how things happen. I think I like her a lot, but she's a little young..."

"How young?" I asked.

He groaned, then laughed, then said, "Very young."

"Under thirty?"

"You might say way under thirty."

"Sounds like Sicilian lightning to me!" I told him. "Is she legal? Fifteen will get you twenty, you know."

He laughed again, and said, "Just out of high school. I think she has a birthday coming up."

"Great," I told him. "You can take her to Serendipity for ice cream. You never know what may happen, pal. You're still a kid at heart. What's her name?"

"Shoshanna," he said, like he was charmed by the beauty of the name.

I could hear in Jerry's voice how far gone he was. It wasn't a dalliance on his part. Maybe it was a Jewish version of getting hit by the unpredictable bolt of Sicilian lightning. Love at first sight. I knew it had to be serious and I just told him to watch out for himself.

It had been years since I'd seen him lose his heart, and this was the only time that I could remember Jerry being willing to put himself in jeopardy. He usually liked to play it safe, but he was willing to risk a lot for this girl, who quickly proved to be more than his match.

Jerry was thirty-nine and the tabloids soon had a field day with his budding relationship to Shoshanna Lonstein. Among those who lampooned him was Howard Stern, who staged some inane gags at Jerry's expense, leading up to a Pay-Per-View New Year's Eve show going into 1994. After that night, Jerry characterized Howard as an "amusing idiot" and they were no longer on speaking terms at all. Allowing the tabloids to have some fun was part of what Jerry called being "a full-service entertainer." It went with the territory. But the feud between the two was one of the few times I'd seen Jerry hurt publicly, and I felt for him, and for Shoshanna.

Of course, we were rooting for them. The next year my wife sent a note to encourage Jerry in the romance, saying in part, "Marry her, marry her—it's genuine and true. She loves you!"

* * *

I think part of the reason that I welcomed his relationship with Shoshanna was that it somehow felt easier for me to lose Jerry's companionship to a woman than write him off to Hollywood and the show. After he became involved with Shoshanna, we saw and heard from him less often on his New York visits, though he did always manage to stay in touch. When he wasn't devoting himself to the romance, he had the show to write and plan, commercials to film, and personal appearances to make, as well as occasional TV specials and club dates.

Still, he was always with us on Thursday nights. This was more and more something of a great joke to the old gang, usually at my expense, when George would bring some new embarrassment or bit of infamy to the Costanza name. My unlucky encounters with casting directors who were looking for Costanza-types

112

proved to be a source of constant disappointment. I tried to get this across to Jerry on the phone one day, but only managed to tell him that the auditions I went to looked like "bald conventions" as I was being typecast. On the famous episode that followed Jerry and George casting their NBC sitcom, *Jerry*, the phrase "bald convention" would come back to vex me when it was used to describe the ragtag group of hairless actors auditioning for the role of George ("The Pilot," May 20, 1993).

When I saw Kramer's buffoonery as a Macy's Santa Claus in "The Race" at the height of the 1994 Christmas season, I was inspired to take my toddling daughters, Mariel and Emily, to visit the tree at Rockefeller Center. The *Seinfeld* production schedule had ended the ritual for Jerry and me, but it was pleasant and somehow reassuring to think back. I decided once a year was probably enough as far as letting nostalgia tug at the heartstrings this way.

At about this time I started jotting down some notes to myself about George. I kept a yellow pad by my bed and wrote down some of those peculiar traits and little moments of shared memory that Jerry had dipped his pen into. I thought about how intensely he worked when he was writing. It was almost like he was in a trance, and I wondered how much of me was consciously in his mind when he thought up jokes and story lines for George as Jerry brainstormed with Larry David and the other writers on the show.

They say that God is in the details, and it was often the tiny details that friends and relatives insisted on asking me about each week. After the first five years the series had been airing, these were some of the pieces of the George puzzle I collected on my night table:

- George is bald. I am bald.
- George is stocky. I am stocky.
- George and I both went to Queens college with Jerry.
- George's high school gym teacher nicknamed him "Can't-Stand-Ya." So did mine.

• George has a thing about bathrooms and parking spaces. So do I. I know I can drive and park better than George, and I think Jerry would admit to this.

• George is sexually right-handed, and must sit on the right of his dates in order to have free access to make a pass. So am I locked into this approach. Because of an old high school football injury, my right hand is limited in its mobility. As I told Jerry many times, I have to have right-hand access on a date, or I might as well take an ice-cold shower.

• George's parents (Jerry Stiller and Estelle Harris) are doubles for my parents.

• Like me, George wasn't allowed to move his father's car when his father had it parked in a good spot. Jerry knew about this strict Costanza policy only too well.

• Both George and I have tried toupés with less than happy results. Jesse says we are "enfollically forlorn."

• Both George and I have worn our ski-lift tickets to impress girls off the slopes, even if we are not quite as lucky at sweeping them off their feet.

• George chooses clothes to fit his mood, as do I. Did Jerry remember this when he saw me in L.A.? Is that why he later gave this bit to George in "The Trip, Part I?"

• Both George and I have experience scalping tickets, waiting with Jerry to be seated at Chinese Restaurants, and going to Yankee games and the U.S. Open.

• Both George and I believe in the code—live by it, die by it!

• George and I came up with the observation that Jerry's show was about "nothing," and we suggested this to Jerry.

• George and I worked in real estate.

• George and I worked as hand models.

• George, Jerry, and I hate working normal jobs, and will go to extreme lengths to avoid them.

• George and I live our lives according to Murphy's Law—we are experts at making things go wrong whenever possible, at "pulling a Costanza."

• George and Jerry adopted my Queens College "Mr. Excitement" motto—"Gotta go, gotta get back, gotta leave."

• Both George and I know what to expect to hear when we buzz Jerry's apartment—"Come on up."

• As Jerry knows, Daily News sports columnist Mike Lupica is a favorite writer for George and me.

• Both George and I now know that "to come up for coffee" is a euphemism for sex, and Jerry will remember what a difficult lesson this was for me to master.

• Both George and I eat peanut butter right out of the jar with our fingers. Jerry knows this. It is the kind of thing that would drive him crazy if I ever did it in his apartment because he would be terrified where I might leave my fingerprints.

It was a game and not a solution to anything. When I became tired of the list, I wrote one question at the bottom of the page: "Would George Costanza exist if I hadn't been born?"

The answer to this question now seems like a mystery wrapped inside a riddle wrapped inside one of Jerry's fortune cookies.

* * *

It was like George had been taken over by an alien. He was turning into a heartless little monster. He was funny, and often sidesplittingly so, but George couldn't have been me when he was relieved to find out his fiancée was dead from licking the cheap wedding invitations he'd insisted upon, poisoned by the glue.

"Why is he like that?" I asked Marie.

"Ask Jerry," she said.

Yes, I heard it from the gang: "Hey, Mike, how much did you pay for those wedding invitations? Where did Jerry get that stuff about you?"

Suddenly, I was a cheap, callous bastard. Still, it brought some drama into my life.

The Jerry-Shoshanna show continued visibly throughout

115

1995 and 1996, and when the guys would call me to ask about Jerry, they also asked if he was "still with what's-her-name." He was, as Shoshanna transferred from George Washington University to UCLA to be closer to him. The two of them would be seen together attending the various award shows that Jerry went to on his way to collecting almost as many Emmys and Golden Globes as he had sneakers. None of us guys would ever have confessed to being jealous of Shoshanna, of course. The code was the code.

Jerry was faithful about calling at the end of each season and it seemed like each year I would hear some bizarre tale about Larry David's latest ranting resignation. It was clear that Larry was pretty hard for Jerry to handle. I kidded him about keeping "the hand" (meaning "the upper hand")—which was another of those buzzword phrases from our youth that applied to so many situations.

On December 30, 1995, the day before New Year's Eve, Jerry came into town for another appearance on Letterman's show, and he called to let us know. I asked if I could get two tickets to the taping for me and my brother, Joe, who was in for the holidays. "They'll be waiting at the box office," said Jerry. Marie agreed to watch the kids for the day, so I took off early with Joe, although I had some misgivings.

I had ballooned to over three hundred pounds at the time, and I wasn't feeling great about myself—it might not have been the best moment for me to connect with Jerry. He hadn't seen me in a while, and I was a little embarrassed—those who have struggled with the fat demon will know what I mean. Still, an opportunity to hang out with Jerry again shouldn't be passed up. My brother Joe was actually tipping the scales more than I was, and the two of us looked very formidable. Wearing our thick winter coats, we might have been mistaken for a couple of mob heavies, instead of the truly innocent, fun-loving guys that we were.

So, at a combined weight of almost 750 pounds, the two of us were an impressive sight walking up Broadway to the Ed Sullivan Theatre. Before they let us in, we stood outside for about a half-hour just watching our breath turn into white clouds. The weather inside the theater wasn't much warmer—as those who have been in the Letterman audience know. The chill keeps his crowd awake and clapping just to keep the blood flowing. An usher led us down the aisle to our seats, which were squeezed together like the ones you get when flying coach. We looked like we were sitting on top of each other in a pile-up.

But we were both ready for the show and the excitement was electric when Jerry came on. He wasn't wearing his Nikes, and Joe said in my ear, "Pretty flashy threads," referring to the stylish shirt and jacket that caught his eye.

"No sneakers tonight," I said.

Jerry slayed them with his monologue, then palled around with Dave like they might have been long lost brothers. During a break, I heard a guy sitting behind me try to impress his date by offering her the earth-shattering observation, "He's the real king of comedy now." The fellow was probably right. The audience seemed ready to elect Jerry president. I was amused whenever I overheard strangers making comments about him. I thought to myself, *if only they knew the half of it.*

Another ovation. Afterward, we headed backstage to see him and were told by a production assistant that we had to go outside and around to the back of the theater to the stage door. Once we found our way outside, we were confronted by a crowd, like it was New Year's Eve in Time's Square. Policemen on horses were trying to keep things under control. Joe and I figured that we'd never make it as far as the door, but we decided to brave it and started pushing through, each of us saying, "Excuse me, please."

It was a miracle. The crowd parted when a guy yelled, "Hey, look out! They're Jerry's bodyguards!"

I played along and tried to sound official. "Let us through, please. We're here to see Mr. Seinfeld."

Suddenly, people hurried aside to clear the way and we had a red carpet to the stage door. With the crowd watching, we banged on the door. A guard opened up, and I convinced him to take our names inside.

A few minutes later Jerry stepped warily out the door. When he saw me, he smiled and quickly gave me a hug. He didn't have to say anything about the weight. He could see easily enough. A few rowdy characters in the crowd called his name out, and he said to me, "I'd better get back inside. Come in for a minute, guys."

We huddled behind the door and I congratulated Jerry for the killing performance. "Another notch on the old gun," I said. Then I asked him, with some hesitation, if he wanted to head out and hit a restaurant. This had been our usual ritual after his shows. The scene was a little awkward for me. The weight. The crowd outside. The two of us standing nose to nose in the drafty hallway of the theater.

Jerry said, "No, I've got some people I have to see tonight, Mike..."

We hugged and said our good-byes, and when Joe and I went back outside, I felt just the slightest twinge of sorrow on top of everything else, a hurt that I couldn't quite put my finger on, and decided it was nothing.

Or almost nothing.

It reminded me of a bit Jerry did on the show ("The Keys") when Elaine and George muttered things under their breath that Jerry couldn't quite hear. He kept wanting to know what each had said, becoming frustrated in his efforts to catch their words, finally accusing them in his bewilderment: "Something. I know it was something..."

I was bewildered too. I still didn't realize or admit to myself how far we'd come, and how far he'd gone.

* * *

In the summer of 1996, *Seinfeld* was flying higher than ever and, in the middle of July, Marie and I invited Jerry and the gang to celebrate Jesse's birthday at our house on Long Island. It was an annual affair, but a difficult time for Jerry to attend because, by now, he was usually heading back to L.A. for a new season. Still, we hoped. I had been going to the gym everyday and had dropped a hundred pounds. I spent hours on the treadmill while watching *Rosie O'Donnell* in the morning and *Oprah* in the afternoon. I was feeling like my old self again, and really looking forward to Jerry making the scene this year. He had never been out to our house.

We were in the backyard and the kids were playing under the Mickey Mouse sprinkler. I had just vacuumed the pool and applied the chlorine and baking soda, fulfilling some of my usual duties as king of the Costanza castle. Marie and one of her friends had been marinating shrimp and salmon steaks for the grill. Brushing a few dark locks of hair off her forehead, she explained the menu to her friend, Leslie, "It's all Jerry food—pasta salad and focaccia with sun-dried tomato, grilled vegetables, grilled shrimp and salmon. Not a fattening thing in sight. Except the birthday cake—made with cannoli cream for Jesse."

Standing with them on the patio, I heard the back gate and thought at first it might be Jerry.

"Hi-ya, bud," came a familiar voice.

It was Tony D'Alto. We hugged and kissed each other on the cheek, which was the custom for Italian guys where we came from. I said, "I thought you were Jerry for some reason."

Tony smirked and asked, not without affection, "Is Numb-Nuts coming, or what?"

Tony D and Jerry were the oil and water of the group. They went way back. Tony worked for the state these days, and he liked to stick out his chin and put on an attitude about Jerry sometimes. But Tony meant no harm. So I explained to him, "If he doesn't have to go to L.A. early. He may have to get back to open up shop on the show. We never know with him these days, but he said he'd try to make it, so he'll probably show."

Tony said, "You keep thinking that, Mikey. Maybe someday it will happen."

I was going to ask what he meant, but Marie broke in, greeting Tony and handing him a Corona and lime. She accepted his kiss on the cheek and asked, "How are Joyce and the kids?"

Tony smiled and told us, "The bride is terrific and so are the little ones." Then he added, "Corona, huh?"

Marie said, pointedly, "Yeah, you know, everything's gotta be just right in case the other one shows up."

I said, "Hey, I would do exactly the same thing, even if it was just me showing up!"

I spotted Jesse and his girlfriend, Susan, coming through the gate. Jesse had been down the divorce road a few years before, but seemed to have held up just fine. He was carrying a cooler and some presents for the kids. With a smile as bright as the sunshine, he shouted, "You guys startin' without me?"

Marie yelled back, "Come on, Birthday Boy!"

When Jesse stepped onto the patio, I gave him a hug and said, "Happy birthday, old man. What is it—forty-two?"

"Yeah," he admitted with a groan.

Tony hugged Jesse and said to me, "He don't look a day over forty-seven."

"Look who's talking," said Jesse. "If you're beard was any whiter, you could play Santa Claus!"

Typical banter, missing only Jerry to complete the picture. Marie welcomed Susan with a quick embrace, then handed beers to her and Jesse. With bottle in hand, Jesse turned and asked me, "Did you call him?"

We all knew who he meant. "Yeah," I said, "I was just telling Tony—he said he'd make it out if he didn't have to go back to L.A. early. If he's still in town, he'll be here."

Jesse and Tony exchanged looks.

"What?" I asked.

Tony let it out, "Come on. The closest Jerry's comin' to Holtsville is the Long Island Expressway...in his Porsche on his way to the Hamptons."

"What are you talking about?" I asked him. "What? Why wouldn't he come here? My house isn't good enough? Is that what you think?"

Jesse stepped in. "No, no, Mike. He didn't mean that. It's just, things change..."

I looked at Jesse and asked, "What are you trying to say now, Jesse? I gave him directions. My house is only six blocks off the L.I.E. What's the big deal about our friend stopping by...even if he wanted to go to the Hamptons afterward? I just don't see it. "

Tony said, hotly, "You don't get it. He's in another world, Mike!"

I held up my hands like Tony was pointing a gun at me. Then I said, "Things change, sure...like your beard. But people don't change inside that way."

My wife shut us down. "If you ask me," she said, "you guys are making a little too much out of this. If he comes, he comes." She held up her glass with a smile, saying to us, "This is a party for Jesse. It's his birthday. Here's to those of us who are here to celebrate and have a good time. Too bad for anybody who can't make it. We have a great meal cooking...and anybody who doesn't like it can kiss my grits. Cheers, you guys!"

We clinked our Coronas and settled back in chaise lounges as Marie took the kids into the pool. I sat back and shaded my eyes from the sun, watching it sparkle on the water, hearing the cries and shrieking laughter of my daughters as they splashed. I could smell the charcoal smoke and our food cooking on the grill. Tony was razzing Jesse about his being single, and Marie was yelling a warning to the kids to stay away from the deep end, calling their names, "Mariel! Emily!"

No, I told myself, I wouldn't trade my life with anyone, not even Jerry.

* * *

I knew that he'd come back to town with another batch of L.A. stories and the usual wry complaints about the life he was leading. The 1997 season was tough for him. By this time, Jerry had stopped doing his trademark monologues at the start of each episode because he had run out of new stand-up material. He told me he just didn't have time anymore to invent those bits to fit the story lines. The critics were saying the show had lost its edge and wasn't as funny as it had been. I didn't think that was so, but I could see how Jerry was gradually losing touch with his roots.

How was he to keep a show about New York City alive when he was no longer here to draw its energy? It was like he'd used up all his memories. Many of his old pals and the life he had once lived on the circuit were gone. I suspected he was out of juice and didn't know it. His edge always came from his stand-up act, and that had to be languishing to some extent without the maddening stimulation and social life of New York.

I called Jerry in April and he told me the news that he had broken up with Shoshanna. He said he had proposed to her, and she had wanted him to leave the show. She was apparently more ready to think about things like building a family and having a home than he was. The story came out in a rush and I heard a lot of emotion in his voice, even when he tried to joke about the breakup and rationalize it, saying, "The problem with her is she's the kind of girl who thinks that when I say I'll be right back that I really will be right back!"

I felt for him. He'd been seeing her for five years and she had given him something nobody else had. We agreed to get together when he came to town the following week. The Jerry on the show had once identified the phrase "We have to talk" as the four worst words in the English language. But I was hoping we might finally have the chance to talk about things.

At long last, a heart-to-heart.

True to his word, Jerry called, and on the Spanish holiday *Cinco de Mayo*, I drove into Manhattan in the morning and found him at his place in the Wendover. He opened the door, and we embraced like the old pals we were. It felt good. The sparse decor hadn't changed and I didn't notice any new additions to the bookshelves. It was a glorious day outside the windows, with buttery patches of sunlight splotching the living room floor.

I tossed a little bag I'd brought along on the couch. Jerry padded through the room in his white Nikes, trying to decide on a shirt. He asked me, "What do you think?"

It was a checkered number, like I remembered him wearing

when we were still in college. He made a face. I said, "It looks good. What's wrong with it?"

"I don't know. I'm not a checkered kind of guy."

He finally settled on it, then sat down, seeming a bit antsy. I reminded him about a time in college when I had broken up with a steady girlfriend, and he and his old flame, Karen, had given me a stuffed animal to cheer me up. With that tale as my introduction, I pulled a tiny stuffed clown out of my bag and handed it to him, saying, "I just wanted to say...I know how it feels, pal."

He had a great laugh, then told me the story again. At the end, he shrugged his shoulders, saying, "I emptied out Tiffany's for her...and she yells at me."

He was still carrying the torch. I looked around the living room and the thought came to me that if I had to get over a woman, this would be the place I'd want to do it. I didn't say anything like that to Jerry. Nor did I ever pry.

He put the clown on the bookshelf, then asked me, "Shall we have a change of scenery? Breakfast? I've got a few errands to run."

"Sounds good," I told him.

Jerry brought his laundry to drop off. Neither of us was in a rush. We walked into a card store, and he took his time picking out Mother's Day cards for his mom and sister. I hadn't seen them in years and was glad to hear they were well. Family was a theme that kept popping up between us.

When we came out of the store, we stopped for a moment to chat with a couple of guys on a stoop who recognized him. Heading along the sidewalk, Jerry looked around at me and said, "It's great to be back here!"

He told me about an American Express commercial he was working on. It was his idea to cast himself with an animated Superman, and to have the two of them strolling along the street.

"Great! You and Superman. A couple of old buddies like us," I couldn't resist saying, just to get a laugh.

Jerry proceeded to act out the commercial for me, showing me how he would soon rescue Lois Lane with his magic AmEx card—an ad first intended for the 1998 Super Bowl audience. The joke came down to Superman having no pockets to carry his credit cards, and I told him, "Sounds like another winner."

Jerry dropped his laundry in a little mom-and-pop store where an ancient Chinese woman smiled up at him and listened patiently to specific instructions on his shirts. Back in the sunshine, we were practically skipping along the sidewalk. People turned their heads as we passed. This was the neighborhood where so many of his jokes had come from.

A guy with a pushcart, yelled, "Hey, Jerry. I love the show! You should put me on, man."

Jerry muttered a polite thanks-but-no-thanks, and I asked him, "Does that happen all the time?"

He said, "You should hear what they say sometimes. Everybody has some great idea for the show that they have to tell me. Here, you be me..."

Suddenly, I was Jerry, and he was racing around me, tugging on my arm, saying, "Jerry, Jerry, I got one for you! Why don't ya have George fall in love with a lady cop? Only she turns out to be a transvestite...think about it, huh?"

He did several imitations of other would-be scriptwriters and had me howling until I had to beg him to stop. People thought we were crazy, but he had a license.

We walked to a little diner at 80th Street and Amsterdam. When we went inside, I noticed the sudden looks of recognition on the faces of the cashier and waitresses, and the other patrons as we found a table. A waitress was already fluttering over us when we sat down. I said to Jerry, "I love going out with you these days just for the service."

He ordered salmon with egg whites, explaining to me, "I asked my nutritionist what kind of food a guy like me needs. Egg whites for high energy. You should try some."

I said, "I'm still watching my weight, but in honor of *Cinco de Mayo*, I'll have the quesadillas."

Jerry asked, "What's *Cinco de Mayo*?"

"What?" I said. "You don't know *Cinco de Mayo*?"

I explained it to him, and we agreed to honor the occasion for this little reunion. We ate and indulged in a lot of guy talk. He told me the series was getting to him, but not because of the barbs from critics. He claimed to be immune. Teflon Jerry. He told me, "I'm getting a little tired of it all, Mikey. Whatever you do in life, you have to enjoy it, right?" I figured Shoshanna had him thinking about things. We kicked around the romance again, and it seemed to me, reading between the lines, that he still hadn't given up on her.

This was the first inkling I had of what was to come.

I said, "It must be hard for you now, making new friends, or just getting to know someone, when everybody relates to you as the person they see on the show. How does anybody really know who you are anymore, Jerry?"

He admitted it was a problem and said the only new friend that he'd made in the last few years was a guy who, like himself, happened to love Porsches.

I asked him, "That's what you have in common?... Porsches?"

"Yeah," said Jerry. "He's a great guy. You know, it's only with women that we need to have absolutely nothing in common. With guys it's different."

This sounded a bit like Zen and the Art of Porsche Maintenance. I teased him, saying, "I think you now own as many Porsches as the number of cars I've had in my whole life."

My junkers were still a running gag between us, and we both cackled. It came to me that we had so little in common now, and yet we had shared so much in the past that we were still friends, still making an effort, still living by the code. He said, "This is the best day I've had in a long time, Mikey. Really, you don't know..."

Then he looked up at me and saw tears in my eyes. He said, "What? What is it, Mikey?"

I couldn't hold it back anymore; it all came out of me in a jumble, about what was going on with my family and raising my two daughters, about George and my own injured pride, and about the constant struggle of just being alive.

I said, "I mean, George is such a loser, and people think that I must be him. The 'Lord of Idiots!' That's not me. I'm the father who took his autistic daughter, Mariel, to the Special Olympics two weeks ago and watched her win a medal in the fifty meter race...I'm the daddy who plays horsey with my little Emily...I'm the guy who's been raising a family for the past eight years you've been doing the show...That's who the real Costanza is...I'm not..."

I was getting too choked up. I could hear my wife's voice in the back of my mind telling me that I was being too emotional. But I had so much I wanted to tell him. There was so much we had never talked about. It was like the whole story I've been telling you in this book was right on the tip of my tongue at that moment, gagging me. How could I ever get him to understand in a conversation? How could I ever get it across to him? It was all so crazy and so far beyond anything that I could say.

I stammered, "I'm not George like people think I am..."

He was genuinely mystified, saying, "But, Mikey, how do they know?"

I didn't know what Jerry meant at first. And then it hit me. I said, "Costanza?"

Catching my point, he told me, "I thought it was a funny name, Mikey. I had no idea..."

Between us, this was a moment of recognition, however tenuous it may have been, a simple acknowledgment after all of these many years.

The waitress brought the check. I lightened up, remembering at that moment my old gym teacher's nickname. Jerry was sensitive, and generous with his concern. He tried to help, but neither of us knew how. It was almost a little scary. I took a couple of deep breaths, and the laughter suddenly came back to both of us.

He said, "Are you okay now?"

"Yeah," I said.

Jerry graciously sprang for breakfast with his Platinum AmEx card and we headed out. He walked me to my car and we were both kicking up our heels again on the sidewalk. I had a new, red Ford Explorer, and I'd left it double-parked on a cross street near the Wendover. When we found it, Jerry said, "Nice spot."

"Lucky I wasn't towed," I said, smiling that he noticed. All those parking conversations way back when.

"How many does this make, Mike?" he asked, meaning the number of cars that I had gone through in my life.

"Number thirty-nine, and still counting," I said. "This one's on a lease. Who knows? Maybe it'll last a while just because it's not mine yet. You know me..."

Then we laughed and hugged a final good-bye. I drove back to Long Island, not really satisfied that he understood what I had been trying to say to him back there, not by a long shot, and yet I was certain of the affection.

I might as well call it love.

* * *

Over the next few months, I started writing things down, like a letter to a dear friend. We talked on the phone and I told him that I was going to write a book about the old days. He said he'd be curious to see what I thought about those times we had. I knew that Jerry liked to write everything himself. His memories were a bag of gold that he had used to advantage for years. But I had my own bag of gold, my own life to recount, my own version of reality as it went down between us.

* * *

On Christmas Eve of 1997, Jerry shocked NBC and the world by announcing he was pulling the plug on *Seinfeld*. This would be his last season and he planned to retire all of his old stand-up routines as well. I hadn't been forewarned, but the news didn't really come as a surprise. The bombshell front-page stories appeared in all of New York City's newspapers. My reactions were very emotional, and I suppose they must have colored much of this book, which I was in the middle of writing with the hope it would bring peace of mind. Only time will tell.

My wife, Marie, said simply, "Thank God, it's over."

I really didn't know what to say. I guess I've said almost all of it here. This is where I'm content to leave it with Jerry, having drawn the fine lines of distinction between me and George, at least for the Costanza family.

At the beginning of the New Year, Jerry revealed his plan to come back to New York. With typical Jerry wit, he said he wanted to get married and have children, noting this might be a little difficult without having a girlfriend. Will any of us be surprised when we hear all about it in his next show? Will we laugh and find whimsical delight in the world, the way that he does when he looks at it for us? I know I will. I'll say, "Welcome home, buddy. It's about time."

* * *

After finishing this last page, I told my wife not to rush out to celebrate too quickly. After all, George will be with us on the reruns for many, many years to come.

Author's Note

The persons in this book are real, but it should be mentioned that I have changed the names of a few of them and altered their descriptions in order to protect their privacy. Although this is a work of nonfiction, I have taken certain storytelling liberties, for example, with the timing and placement of some events. Where the narrative strays from strict nonfiction, my intention has been to remain faithful to the characters and to the essential drift of the scenes and events as they really happened, to the best of my recollection.

MIKE COSTANZA is an actor who has appeared onstage in several off-off-Broadway productions, in television commercials and films. He also works as a Realtor on Long Island. He lives in Holtsville, NY with his wife, Marie, and their two daughters, Mariel and Emily. This is his first book.

GREG LAWRENCE is also the co-author
of *Dancing on My Grave*, the best-selling
autobiography of ballerina Gelsey
Kirkland, and *The Shape of Love* (both
published by Doubleday and Berkley
Books). He lives in Manhattan and is a
co-founder of WordWise Literary
Services. He is pictured here with publisher Bonnie Egan.

THE REAL SEINFELD
AS TOLD BY THE REAL COSTANZA

ORDERING INFORMATION

INDIVIDUALS
Pathway Book Service
Gilsum, NH 03448

Phone: 1 (800) 345-6665
E-Mail: pbs@top.monad.net

BOOKSTORES AND LIBRARIES
Distributor to the trade:
Access Publishers Network
6893 Sullivan Road, Grawn, Michigan 49637
Phone: (616) 276-5196
                (800) 345-0096 FAX (800) 950-9793

PUBLISHER
WordWise Literary Services
WordWise Books
65 Second Avenue New York, NY 10003-8616

Phone: (212) 473-8281 FAX (212) 505-6005
E-Mail: wordwiseb@aol.com

WEBSITE
http://members.aol.com/wordwiseb/realcostanza/